Why Be a Temp?

- To be free to *Work When You Want to Work!*
- To earn cash to pay bills, tuition, buy a car, take a trip—or save money.
- To explore different professions before selecting a career.
- To avoid the boredom of the same job.
- To learn a new skill—or sharpen your present ones.
- To supplement a fixed income.
- To be independent, self-confident and productive!

JOHN FANNING is founder and president of Uniforce Temporary Personnel, Inc., and an influential leader in the personnel field.

WORK When You Want to WORK

The Complete Professional Guide for the Temporary Worker

by John Fanning
President of
Uniforce Temporary Personnel, Inc.
with George Sullivan

PUBLISHED BY POCKET BOOKS NEW YORK

POCKET BOOKS, a division of Simon & Schuster, Inc.
1230 Avenue of the Americas, New York, N.Y. 10020

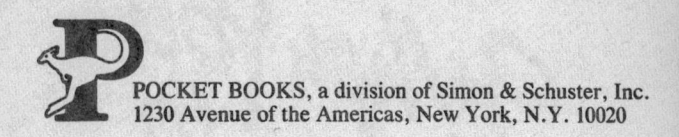

Copyright © 1985 by John Fanning and George Sullivan
Cover artwork copyright © 1985 Pocket Books

All rights reserved, including the right to reproduce
this book or portions thereof in any form whatsoever.
For information address Pocket Books, 1230 Avenue
of the Americas, New York, N.Y. 10020

ISBN: 0-671-52561-1

First Pocket Books printing July, 1985

This is a revised edition of *Work When You Want to Work*
by George Sullivan,
originally published in 1969 by Collier Macmillan,
A Division of Macmillan Publishing Company, Inc.

10 9 8 7 6 5 4 3 2

POCKET and colophon are registered trademarks
of Simon & Schuster, Inc.

Printed in the U.S.A.

This book is dedicated to all the people who work "temporary" and touch my life every day.

—JOHN FANNING

Author's Note

This book profiles real people and recounts their experiences. Some of the names have been changed to provide anonymity for those who requested it.

Contents

1	"No More Boring Jobs"	13
2	Why Temp Work? Dollar and Psychic Income	27
3	Be Your Own Talent Scout	37
4	Opening the Door	47
5	Call Today—Temp Tomorrow	53
6	Unleashing Your Talents	69
7	Becoming a Super Temp Is Easy	83
8	You and Your Paycheck	97
9	Temp Solutions	109
10	Crisis Temping	117
	Suddenly Unemployed	120
	Moonlighting	124
	Temporary Jobs for the Retired	127
	Temp Your Way Through College	132
11	Maximizing Your Options	139
12	The Temp World—Excitement and Personal Growth	161
	Job Descriptions	167
	Glossary	187

WORK When You Want to WORK

1
"No More Boring Jobs"

Mrs. Ellen Tymon, a 34-year-old homemaker, is working the next two weeks as an executive secretary for the president of a Long Island toy manufacturer. David Liebman, a Chicago college student, is employed every Saturday as a telephone solicitor for a magazine subscription agency. Ed Wakin, a 26-year-old aeronautical engineer, recently completed four months employment with a major California aircraft manufacturer and plans a four-week vacation before taking on his next assignment.

These three people have one thing in common: they are all "temporaries"—members of a growing army of people who work when they want to work and for as long as they want. This situation, however idyllic it may seem, is simple for any person to achieve. It's merely a matter of becoming hired by a temporary-help service.

Ellen Tymon's case is somewhat typical of those returning to the work force for other than purely financial reasons. When her only child entered high school, Ellen found herself with too much free time during the day. She had tired of PTA service long ago and was bored with volunteer work. All of Ellen's relatives, outside of her husband and daughter, were back in Ohio, and she didn't have many close friends. "So what was I going to do," she asked, "go shopping every day?"

Ellen finally decided to go back to work. Before her marriage she was an executive secretary with a large firm in a job she found quite easy to handle. But now she didn't want to work full time. "I felt it would be too tough a grind. I didn't want any part of running a home while working a full-time, 9 a.m. to 5 p.m. job," she said. Her husband also objected to full-time employment for her, fearing that the extra income might put them in a higher tax bracket.

Once it was agreed that Ellen could return to work, she worried that her secretarial skills would be too rusty. In the twelve years that she was at home, her typing was kept fairly current through regular use of a portable typewriter on which she wrote letters to friends. Her shorthand, which she had not used at all, had left her life completely. "I needed shorthand to be an executive secretary, which pays a lot better than a typist," she noted. "So I went through my high school shorthand book, chapter by chapter, for one hour a day. It took four months, but at the end of that time I knew my outlines."

Even though she regained confidence in her skills, Ellen was still apprehensive about what lay ahead. She agonized over the uncertainties of job interviews and suffered butterflies in her stomach whenever she thought about working in a new place. "Then I realized the only way to drive away that anxiety was to go for an interview, get hired, and go to work."

"And that's exactly the way it happened," she said. "I went to the temp service that had been advertising in a local paper, was evaluated, and the next day they had me working as an executive secretary." Everything went fine at the job, and by the second or third day she felt like she belonged there.

Since signing on with Uniforce Temporary Services about ten years ago, Ellen has worked for 127 different companies (she keeps count). Her skills are in great demand, so she's able to be very selective about her assignments: one-day jobs are rejected, two five-day weeks are her favorite. "I'll stretch out an assignment for six or seven weeks if I like the place and they really need me," she said. "But I won't take an assignment that's more than a 30-minute drive from my home."

After finishing an assignment, Ellen takes a few weeks off. "I make my own clothes, and my daughter's too, so I go shopping for fabric and do some sewing. Or I might do nothing at all—whatever *I* decide."

The Temp Workstyle

Besides "empty nesters" like Ellen Tymon, mothers of school-age children often seek out temping jobs because it allows them to be home when the youngsters arrive. They can also take summers off when the kids are on vacation.

It's this flexibility, and freedom to decide when you want to work that is the most appealing aspect of working as a temp. "As a permanent employee, I always felt as if I were 'married' to the company," says one temp worker. "And it took a 'divorce,' with all the associated trauma, to get free again.

"But it's not like that when you're a temp. You set your own course. You feel liberated."

Another benefit of temping is that your work environment can change from one week to the next, or even from one day to the next. You're always meeting new people and making new friends. One temp puts it this way: "I'm a good typist, and it's easy for me to get permanent secretarial work—but it's boring. So, the only way I ever do secretarial work is as a temp. Things are seldom dull when you're temping. You're always meeting different people. There are no more boring jobs."

Many of our employees have told us that they enjoy temping because there is no pressure once you leave the job. "You go to work, do your job, and go home," says one. "You never get so involved that you bring your job home with you."

"The responsibility is always someone else's," says a 28-year-old clerk-typist, a temporary employee for eight years. "When I go home at night, I want to leave the job behind."

Temping is well suited to a multitude of modern lifestyles. College students and temping go together like pizza and soda. Students like temping because they can adjust their work schedules to suit their class schedules. During summer vacations, when temporary-help offices throughout the country are flooded with students, temporary employment is considered their principal source of income, and many return to their favorite temp service every summer.

Moonlighters, those individuals who work an additional job, choose temping because of the flexible work hours. If they want to work at night, after they're finished with their full-time jobs, they can do so. If they want to work only in the months before Christmas (as many do), they can do that, too.

Actors and actresses and dancers and musicians often temp in order to support themselves between performing jobs.

Retirees are another group who often work as temps, particularly those women and men who have found their retirement incomes are insufficient for their daily needs. Temping can also help to relieve their boredom and provide the calendar quarters of employment that are needed to qualify for Social Security benefits (see Chapter 10).

It's a fast-growing trend: newly graduated students are temping in order to explore different businesses or different companies while making up their minds about their careers. In other words, they use temp work as a steppingstone to permanent employment. "It gives you the opportunity of meeting different people, of getting to know different kinds of companies," says one student. "It's like peeking into windows."

More and more of our temps are permanent-job seekers. They are temping to explore a particular field or a particular company. "It's a marvelous way to look for a permanent job," says one. "It enables you to 'try before you buy.' You find out whether you like the people with whom you're working. You find out what working conditions are like and what kind of money the company pays."

No matter what your motivation happens to be, this book will help you sample the temping lifestyle. It is based upon my more than two decades of experience as the head of a national temporary-help firm, upon the knowledge my associates and I have gathered from interviewing and placing thousands of women and men in temporary-help jobs.

The book is intended to make it clear that the temporary-help industry has the welcome mat out for you. It examines how temp services work; it gives you an insider's view of what happens during interview and evaluation processes. It explains how to become a successful—super—temp worker. And it offers career and educational information to help you improve your skills or develop new ones.

One thing that I've come to understand is that many women approach the idea of work outside the home with assorted fears and conflicts. This book is meant to help you overcome those feelings, to start you moving, to get you through the door. Once you've accomplished that, you'll find the rest is easy.

Temping—What It Is

A temporary-help employee, often called a "temp," is an individual who is recruited and hired by a temporary-help service, then assigned to one of the service's client companies for a couple of days, a week, a month or even several months. When it is over, the temp is offered another assignment. The temp is never charged a fee.

The client company pays the temporary-help service an agreed-upon rate per hour per employee, with the rate directly related to the employee's skill and experience. The temporary-help service pays the temp and makes the standard deductions for withholding tax, Social Security and the like.

A temp can accept or reject assignments as they are offered. Temps work when they want to work for as long as they want.

As this implies, the temporary-help firm is entirely different from the employment agency. The employment agency is a job broker. Once you, the job seeker, have been placed in a permanent position, the employment agency has done its job. You have no further relationship with it.

In the case of the temporary-help firm, you maintain a continuing relationship with the firm. You are under their direction; you are their employee.

What It Is Not

Don't confuse temporary work with "part-time" work. Part-time work is often permanent. A part-time worker might be the individual who works as a supermarket cashier on Friday nights and all day Saturdays. Such a person is a regular employee of the company; she or he is likely to work the same hours each week on the same days for perhaps as many as 50 weeks out of the year.

Temporary employees work at a variety of companies, and choose the number of days they work each week. The hours they work can vary from week to week.

Temporary employment has nothing to do with job sharing, the arrangement by which two employees hold one position, dividing the duties and responsibilities and, of course, the salary and fringe benefits.

Job sharing is very similar to part-time work; it is an idea that is growing in popularity in both small and large companies. But job sharing has little flexibility to it: You work an agreed-upon number of hours each week and always for the same company.

Growth and Change

The temporary-help industry is made up of more than a thousand companies that operate over 4,500 offices in the United States and Canada. In one recent year, these firms employed more than 4 million women and men, and generated over $5 billion in sales.

As recently as the early 1960s, less than a half million individuals were employed by all temporary-help companies combined. However, by the end of the decade, the industry had doubled in size. Then it doubled in size again.

Not only is the temporary-help industry flourishing now, but it is getting bigger. In the past decade the industry had an annual growth rate that ranged from 17 to 22 percent, according to the National Association of

Temporary Services. And the U.S. Department of Labor has said that the temporary-help field will be one of the fastest-growing industries during the 1980s.

With growth has come change. Whereas businesses once used temporary employees almost solely as replacements for vacationing staff members, they now hire temps to handle the additional work that accompanies special projects or periodic increases in production.

As a result, the nature of temporary work has changed. For example, the duration of individual assignments has gotten longer. It used to be that temps worked only for a few days to a couple of weeks for the client company. But assignments now can last for several weeks, months, even for a year or more.

The biggest change has been in the variety of work available. Jobs in the temp field were once usually limited to typing and filing; while most opportunities for employment continue to be in office work, there is a greater variety of specialized jobs available.

Looking Back

The idea of employing individuals on a temporary basis was first tried in the 1930s, but it didn't begin to take hold until the mid-1940s when business firms saw their office workers enter the armed services during World War II. At the same time thousands of housewives and retirees found themselves with spare time, and they wanted to be able to use that time productively—to earn money. It was logical for a business to be born that would match the demand for skilled workers with the pool of available talent.

When World War II ended, veterans by the millions returned to reclaim their jobs, which, by law, employers had to hold open for them. This was very disruptive to many of the temporary fill-ins who enjoyed working. They liked the extra income it provided. They wanted to continue working.

Thousands of retirees felt the same way. Being idle again held no appeal.

Some of those out-of-work individuals went to employment agencies and asked to be hired a few days each week. But the employment agencies, geared to placing individuals in permanent jobs, were unable to place people seeking temporary employment. When the needs of these displaced workers began to be recognized, the concept of the temporary-help service took a firmer hold.

The temporary-help services office of the 1940s was primitive by today's standards. It was usually only a one- or two-person operation, and supplied women (rarely men) for basic office tasks—clerical and secretarial work.

The earliest pioneers of a temporary-help service were two Minneapolis lawyers who foresaw the opportunities the industry offered. The company they founded got its start one day in 1948 when the two men were in a desperate need of secretarial help to prepare a legal brief. One of the men, Elmer L. Winter, happened to think of a former secretary of his who had married, then left the firm to have a baby. He called the woman and asked whether she would be willing to return to work for a day or two. The woman agreed to come back and the crisis was averted.

Later it occurred to Winter and his partner, Aaron Scheinfeld, that their experience had not been an isolated case. Surely there were other law firms and business offices where skilled help was often needed on an "instant" basis. A check with friends and colleagues showed this to be true. The two founded a company that provided temporary help to businesses and industries. They called the firm Manpower. Today, of course, it is one of the giants of the temporary-help field.

Although simple and austere by standards of today, the first temporary services had the same basic characteristics as the modern temp firm. They recruited and hired individuals, then rented them out at hourly rates to client companies. Employees of these firms liked the idea of having their assignments arranged for them, with the matter of wages settled in advance, and not having to pay a fee for these services. They also liked the idea of being able to choose between each assignment as it was offered.

Advantages to the Client

Businesses and industries have also found many benefits in using temporary workers. Savings can be achieved by not having to pay fringe benefits (since the temp worker is an employee of the temp service, not the client company). In addition, temps are paid only for the work performed, whereas permanent employees are paid for unproductive time, sick days and vacation days. Businesses also save on the extra charges incurred through overtime.

By having access to a skilled bank of fully trained personnel, the client company is able to maintain a leaner, more efficient permanent staff. The firm is also able to eliminate expensive and time-consuming recruiting procedures.

One reason for the temporary-help industry's enormous growth in recent years is the realization by the business community that temporary help can be used to save money and increase productivity through a program of balanced staffing. This means keeping a company's permanent staff to a minimum throughout the year, then supplementing it with temporaries to handle work peaks. According to a survey conducted by Uniforce in 1984, approximately 58 percent of our client companies use balanced staffing techniques.

Take the potato-chip industry as an example. The manufacture of potato chips is somewhat seasonal in nature: Demand for chips is the greatest just before the year-end holidays and the Super Bowl. So toward the end of the year, we begin supplying workers to potato-chip companies. They're used chiefly for quality control, seeking out bad potatoes and chips. It would be wasteful for these firms to be staffed for peak production the year round.

Another radical change in the temp-help industry is in the variety of jobs now available. While it's still true that most temps work in office and clerical jobs as secretaries, typists, data processors and clerks, more and more workers are being placed in other fields.

One of the fastest-growing areas is the health-care field. Temp services now provide registered nurses, licensed practical nurses, home health aides and dentists' assistants for work in hospitals, nursing homes, private offices and residences.

There's also been a significant growth in the marketing divisions of some temp services. These supply women and men to staff trade-show booths, to work as interviewers and product demonstrators, to distribute fliers, to conduct sampling programs in department stores and supermarkets—and to work as Santas at Christmas and Easter bunnies in the spring.

All the major temp services have light industrial divisions, providing people to assemble, solder, sort, pack, wrap, count, stamp, label, test, inspect and perform many other such tasks. Some have technical divisions for engineers, draftspersons, surveyors and writers.

The final section of this book cites and assesses many of the jobs being offered by temp services.

One other recent change is one of image. A temporary worker often used to be looked upon as one who wasn't quite qualified to hold a permanent job. Not anymore. "The agencies no longer turn out a slipshod work force with little or no training in a limited number of fields," said a recent article in *Administrative Management* magazine. ". . . Quality has become the foremost attribute of the temporary employee."

As the industry entered the 1980s, the demand for temps was at an all-time high. "There was always work," says an Anaheim, California, temp who took time off recently to have a baby. "Sometimes I'd tell them I didn't want to work, but they'd call me anyway. 'We've got a terrific job for you,' they'd say. 'Maybe you'd like to reconsider.' I'd usually end up saying yes."

People in Demand

With companies requesting more and more temps from an ever-increasing number of temp firms, a shortage of temp employees in some skill areas has begun to develop. By the end of the decade, these shortages could be critical.

The temporary-personnel industry has always been a "people" business. We depend on people for our existence, and today our need for people is greater than ever before. To you, the prospective temporary worker, that need translates into opportunity.

2

Why Temp Work? Dollar and Psychic Income

Uniforce and other temporary-help companies ask each prospective employee to complete an application form that contains the following question: "Why are you seeking temporary employment?"

The answers we get have a common theme:

"The money."

"To pay bills."

"I like to eat."

"The pay—I need the money."

"$"

It comes as no revelation to say that the great majority of people who work do so for economic reasons. This holds true for women as well as men. According to a recent survey conducted by *The New York Times*, 32 percent of the women who worked said they did so to support their families; 24 percent stated they worked to support themselves.

To the married woman with a family, the income

from temping often represents an improved standard of living. "We don't have to pinch pennies anymore," is the way one of our employees put it. Those additional dollars may mean better clothes for the youngsters or new furniture.

In other households, the woman's income goes toward luxury items like a second car or a resort vacation. Sometimes it goes into a savings account for emergencies or it helps to pay college tuition for a son or daughter. In recent years, we had many instances of women working to accumulate money for an IRA account.

"I use most of what I earn on household expenses," one woman told me. "But some I just spend extravagantly on myself, my husband or the kids. I just blow it. Everyone should have a little bit of money that they can burn without being held accountable."

Psychic Income

The benefits a woman derives from work outside the home are much more than economic. Working provides what I call "psychic income." Through the feeling of accomplishment and self-improvement she gets out of working, a woman's confidence and self-esteem builds. She becomes a happier person.

Many women have told me that once they take temp jobs their relationship with their husbands improve; their marriage becomes more of a partnership. No longer is the woman regarded as merely a housekeeper and cook; she finds the children appreciate her more.

I don't want to give the impression that working brings perfection to family life. More than a few men have had to deal with insecurity when their wives go out to work. Some resent the demands made upon them to help out with the household chores. Some worry that their wives are going to find their new lives more attractive than their previous ones.

But the benefits more than compensate. Time after time, I've seen women grow in confidence, poise and self-assurance as they move from assignment to assignment, becoming more proficient in old skills and acquiring new ones.

Many of the benefits of "psychic income" were confirmed by a poll conducted by *The New York Times* in 1983. It found that women generally looked upon work and independence as elements of life that were as satisfying as husbands, homes and children.

Based on telephone interviews with 1,309 adult women and men, the poll revealed that 58 percent of American working women would rather work than stay at home—and so would 31 percent of nonworking women.

The importance of work to the American woman was also made clear through follow-up interviews with some of the women surveyed. "My mother got up in the morning, washed clothes, hung them out, and went to the grocery store," the *Times* quoted one woman as saying. "I learned from that if you don't get out there and talk to people every day you're going to get stale."

Getting Trained

Many thousands of women and men have found temping to be a good way of getting introduced to or trained in the use of modern office technology—memory typewriters, call directors and sophisticated copiers.

Countless secretaries and typists have been introduced to word processors through temping. During the early 1980s, many of the major temp-help firms began providing word-processing training. (For more information on word processing, see Chapter 8).

Your Pay

The temporary-help service pays on a weekly basis for the hours you work. It's standard practice for the work week to begin on Monday and end the following Sunday.

The temp service makes all the usual deductions from the total amount earned—federal income tax, Social Security, plus whatever state and city deductions are mandated by law, including those for state taxes and disability insurance, where applicable.

At Uniforce and some other services, each employee maintains her or his own payroll record, or a weekly time card. For each day you're on assignment, you enter the time you started work, the time you finished and the number of hours worked. At the end of the week, you enter the total number of hours (rounded to the nearest quarter), sign the card and have your supervisor sign it. Be sure the card bears the job number (provided by your personnel coordinator) and your Social Security number. Then mail the card to the temporary service, or deliver it if it's more convenient to do so.

In the case of Uniforce, the company's payroll unit in New York processes all time cards and prepares payroll checks. It normally takes employees a week to receive their checks. A few temporary-help services make provisions for employees to receive their checks on the Friday evening of the work week, but this policy is much more the exception than the rule.

Sometimes it's said that the wage rates for temporary employees are generally lower than for permanent employees. Suppose you're a typist. One day you're sent out on an assignment and you learn that the typist at the next desk, doing exactly the same work, is earning more money than you are, even though you seem to be more skilled than the other employee. The difference is that the other typist is a permanent employee. But keep in mind that the permanent employee may have worked for the company for several years, and received annual pay increases. Or the permanent employee may be a beneficiary of a wage scale established by union bargaining.

If you encounter this situation, my advice is not to focus on the difference that exists between your salary and the other typist's, but concentrate instead on how you can increase your own earning power. Seek to upgrade your skills; the more skilled you are as a typist, the more you'll get paid. That's a standard policy in the temporary-work field. Also be aware that most temporary services give merit pay increases to employees for consistently productive work over extended periods.

A similar complaint concerns benefits. It is said that temporary employees lose out on many of the fringes that permanent employees enjoy, particularly medical coverage, but also in the form of pension plans, paid holidays, sick days and retirement funds. While this complaint is valid, it is less valid today than it used to be. More and more, temporary services are offering benefits to their employees. Admittedly, the benefits that you receive from a temporary service are not the equal of what you might get from a permanent employer, but the gap *is* beginning to close.

Related to the subject of benefits is the lack of security that is sometimes cited as one of temping's shortcomings. An employee in a permanent job knows that she or he is going to receive a paycheck this week, next week, the week after, as long as her or his performance meets company standards. The temp, of course, has no such guarantee.

There is not too much that I can say in answer to that complaint. Temporary work is, by its nature, not permanent, so the benefits that accrue to the permanent worker can hardly be made to apply to a temporary employee.

But to the temporary employee who seeks to work steadily, my advice is to register with more than one service. Sign up with two, three or more of them. If you have a marketable skill, there's no reason that you should not be able to work from 9 A.M. to 5 P.M., five days a week, 52 weeks a year.

A final word on the subject of job security: During the recent economic recession, when wholesale layoffs of permanent employees became pandemic and the unemployment rate was shooting through the ceiling, there was no decrease in the demand for temporary workers. Millions of them continued to work as if the recession had not been taking place. Security is not always what, or where, it seems to be.

No Fees

The temporary service will interview you, evaluate your skills, find you a job, negotiate what you are to be paid—and never charge you a fee. The temporary service is paid by the client company, and out of what it receives the service pays its expenses and earns its profit.

Pay Increases

The more assignments you accept and complete successfully, the more experience you gain. Increased experience usually implies improved skills, which means you may be eligible for higher pay. Speak to your personnel coordinator at the temp service when you feel you deserve a pay increase.

Vacation Pay

You also may be entitled to paid vacation days after you've worked a specified number of hours within a certain time. At one service, for example, you're entitled to 2½ days of paid vacation after you've worked 750 hours within a six-month period.

You don't have to take the vacation days after the six months have elapsed. You can continue to accumulate hours, since you are also entitled to five days paid vacation after working 1,400 hours in any 12-month period.

To receive vacation pay, you must keep track of your hours and days worked, and make a formal request for payment to your personnel coordinator. Present the appropriate pay stubs along with your request.

Holiday Pay

One temp service gives its temporary employees an opportunity to receive pay for six holidays—Christmas Day, New Year's Day, Thanksgiving Day, Memorial Day, Independence Day and Labor Day. To be eligible, they must have worked 800 hours during the 12-month period before each holiday, and also have worked the week before and the week after the holiday.

As in the case of vacation pay, temps must make a formal request for holiday pay, presenting pay stubs that document their eligibility.

Talent-Scout Bonuses

Temporary-service companies are constantly searching for skilled and reliable employees. Individuals with office skills are particularly needed. If you know a secretary, stenographer, typist or word processor, and you send that person to the temporary-service firm that you work for, and they're hired, you receive a cash bonus. The higher the skill level of the person you recommend, the bigger the bonus you receive.

At one service you get paid when the person completes her or his first assignment. With some other companies, the new employee has to work an extended period before you receive payment.

Other Benefits

Many temporary-service companies also pay performance bonuses. At one service, for example, if you work 300 hours in any three-month period, you'll receive an extra $20.

To qualify, you must have good punctuality and attendance records and have received satisfactory performance evaluations from the client companies for whom you worked.

Keep in mind that not all temporary-service firms offer the same bonus package. And with some national temporary-personnel companies, in fact, the policies regarding benefits and bonuses vary from one region of the country to another. What applies for one national-service office in Anaheim, California, may not hold true for their offices in Westchester County, New York. Thus, if you switch from one office to another, be sure to establish in advance the extras you are going to be receiving, even though you are working for the same company.

Unemployment Insurance

Unemployment insurance, the protection for people who are out of work through no fault of their own, applies in many states to temporary employees.

Disability Insurance

A few states have laws which provide that persons who cannot work for an extended period of time, due to illness or an off-the-job injury, may collect disability benefits. If your state is one of them, then working as a temporary may qualify you to collect benefits, if you become disabled.

Workers' Compensation Insurance

Should you be injured in the course of your employment, it is likely that your medical bills will be paid, thanks to the workers' compensation insurance program administered by your state. If your injury is disabling, you may be entitled to receive additional benefits.

Employers, including temporary-help services, arrange for the payment of workers' compensation benefits through private insurance companies. The premium is solely the employer's expense; no contribution is ever taken from an employee's wages.

Social Security Benefits

All temporary-help firms provide Social Security coverage; they're legally required to do so. (See Chapter 10 for an explanation of how this coverage can affect your Social Security benefits.)

The deductions from your paycheck that help to subsidize some of the above benefits no doubt seem painful at first glance. But it may ease the sting if you realize that they bring you guaranteed protection against the financial pressure you are almost certain to experience through loss of employment, disabling injury or accident.

3

Be Your Own Talent Scout

The world of temping is an enormous one, and it's changing all the time. Advances in office technology create new jobs; old ones get phased out.

The big problem with people who seek temporary employment is that they don't consider all the jobs for which they're qualified. They usually ask only about those areas in which they have already worked, sharply limiting their opportunities.

This chapter is intended to help you pinpoint the many skills you have and develop as many job possibilities as you can. Don't hesitate to consider areas you might never have thought of before. If your list becomes too long, you can always cut it back.

Begin by reviewing what you've accomplished throughout your life, whether as a homemaker, volunteer worker, employee or student. It's probably easiest to start at the present and work back. Jot down all the facts you feel might be important. You'll end up with an inventory of your background and work experience. (You can also use the inventory to furnish the facts you'll need on an interview and to fill out the application form at the temp service.)

Don't overlook your experience as a homemaker. Personnel specialists agree that a woman whose main occupation has been her home and family is prone to underrate her abilities and talents. The truth is that homemakers have countless skills that have value in the labor market. In managing family finances, for example, a woman is likely to have established monetary goals, set budgets, maintained a checking account, kept financial records and prepared tax forms, all of which should be brought to the attention of the temp service. List any professional assistance you might have provided your spouse, relatives or friends. You may have assisted them in writing reports or preparing speeches.

Your inventory should also include work that you might have performed with volunteer organizations. You may, for instance, have planned, coordinated or directed activities of a group. You may have organized and conducted meetings, given speeches, written reports or trained other volunteers. Sometimes volunteer work involves clerical duties, organizing schedules, or heavy telephone use—all important skills in the temporary-help field.

Your School Record

Going further back, make a note of the schools you attended, the principal courses you took, the year you graduated from each and the degrees or certificates you earned. List every award you ever received and your extracurricular activities while in school.

What about the jobs you held during your school years or the summers between years? List the positions you held and your duties.

Be sure to include any extension courses or adult-education courses you might have taken.

Your Personal Interests

List your personal interests, and note the number of years you've been involved with each activity. For example, are you a person who rides a bicycle two or three times a year, or are you a real enthusiast? Maybe you've organized long-distance bicycle tours or overnight camping trips. If you sew, do you merely mend socks, or do you design your own clothes?

What about your hobbies and leisure-time activities? Often a person's hobby pinpoints what she or he is really interested in. One woman whose hobby was writing has been placed in a job editing manuscripts for a national magazine.

Last, put down the names of all the social groups and professional organizations to which you've belonged. Describe your involvement with each.

Your Job Experience

In making a self-appraisal, devote a separate page to your job experience. List all the work you've done, whether it be full time part time or temporary, paid or unpaid.

Begin with the most recent year in which you were employed, then work in reverse, year by year. For each entry, write down the name of the company or organization for which you worked, the title of the job you held and the skills involved.

Plan to bring your Social Security card. If you don't care to carry the card with you, copy the number onto your personal inventory list.

Determining Your Skills

The lists of skills on the pages that follow (taken from the typical job-application form) are meant to help you focus upon those jobs for which you're most qualified. Go over the lists carefully and check those skills in which you have had training or experience. You may come up with 15 or 20. Jot down the list on a separate paper and bring it to the interview.

Office Skills

TYPING
— Electric
  Make/Model_____
  Make/Model_____
  Make/Model_____
— Electronic
  Make/Model_____
— Other _____
  _____
  _____

MATERIAL
— Addressing
— Billing
— Correspondence
— Manuscript
— Policy/Claim
— Statistical
— Technical

TRANSCRIPTION
— Belt — Disc — Tape
  — Machines _____
  _____
  _____

SECRETARIAL
— Engineering
— Executive
— Legal
— Medical
— Fast Longhand
— Speed Writing
— Steno
   System _____
— Bilingual
   — Speak
   — Steno
   — Translate
   — Type

WORD PROCESSING SYSTEMS
— IBM
— Lanier
— Wang
— Other _____
_____
_____

PERSONAL COMPUTERS
   Make/Model_____
   Make/Model_____
   Make/Model_____

CLERICAL
— Addressing
— Coding
— Collating
— Figures
— Filing
   — Alpha
   — Numerical
— Inventory

- ___ Mailroom
- ___ Microfilm
- ___ Proofreading
- ___ Receptionist
- ___ Telephone
- ___ Other _____

OFFICE MACHINES
- ___ Calculator
- ___ Photocopier
- ___ Teletype
- ___ 10 Key
- ___ Other _____

TELEPHONE EQUIPMENT
- ___ Call Director
- ___ Console
    - Make/Model _____
    - Make/Model _____
    - Make/Model _____
- ___ PBX
- ___ Other _____

BOOKKEEPING
- ___ Accounts Payable
- ___ Accounts Receivable
- ___ Assistant
- ___ Full Charge
- ___ Payroll
    - System _____
- ___ Bank Reconciliation
- ___ General Ledger
- ___ Trial Balance

___ Other _____
_____
_____

DATA PROCESSING
___ Application
___ Computer Operator
    System _____
___ CRT Operator
___ Data Entry
_____
_____

___ Key Punch
___ Key Tape
    Make/Model _____

___ Programmer
    Language _____

MISCELLANEOUS
___ Accountant
___ Bank Teller
___ Cashier
___ Credit & Collection
___ Demonstrator
___ Dental Hygienist
___ Draftsperson
___ Engineer
___ Lab Technician
    Type _____
___ Librarian
___ Nurse
    RN No. _____
    LPN No. _____
___ Production Control
___ Telephone Sales

Be Your Own Talent Scout

__ Other _____

LIGHT INDUSTRIAL WORK
- __ Assembly
    - __ Hand
    - __ Machine
- __ Bagging
- __ Bindery
- __ Bundling
- __ Capping
- __ Carpentry
- __ Collating
- __ Counting
- __ Electrical
- __ Factory Work
- __ Filing
- __ Food Service
- __ Gluing
- __ Hand Tools

_____

- __ Inserting
- __ Inspection
- __ Inventory
- __ Labeling
- __ Lab Technician
    - __ Chemical
    - __ Medical
    - __ Physical
- __ Maintenance Work
- __ Material Handler
- __ Packaging
    - __ Hand
    - __ Machine

- Packing
- Power Tools

_____
_____
_____

- Printed Circuits
- Receiving
- Schematics
- Shipping
- Soldering
- Sorting
- Spray-Painting
- Stamping
- Tagging
- Testing
- Trimming
- Weighing
- Welding
    Type _____
    _____

- Wiring
- Wrapping

DUPLICATING/MAILROOM
- Addressograph
- Collator
- De-collator
- Ditto
- Mimeo
- Multi/Offset
    - B & W
    - Camera
    - Color
- Postage Meter
- Other _____
_____
_____

4
Opening the Door

The best place to learn about the temporary-help services in your area is through the classified advertising section of a local daily or Sunday newspaper. Look in the "Help Wanted" columns under the heading "Temporary" or "Temporary Services." Some temp firms advertise under individual skill categories, such as "Typist," "Clerk" or "Word Processor."

Read the advertisements carefully. Some will be general in nature to attract applicants in wholesale lots, while others will mention specific jobs or job skills. There will be some firms that specialize in office-related jobs, others that have medical jobs available and still others that seek industrial or technical workers.

Sometimes the very name of the temp service tips off the kinds of workers it is seeking. In New York City, for instance, there are temp firms named Office Temporaries and Medi-Temps. International Temporaries hires clerical workers who are bilingual and places them in jobs where the use of more than one language is essential. Salespower, a division of Manpower, Inc., the largest temporary-help company, provides salespersons on a temporary basis.

If you have a special skill that is not mentioned in any of the advertisements, it's a good idea to call several firms to determine in advance those most interested in interviewing you. When you call a company and learn it is not seeking individuals in your skill area, ask the company representative to recommend a firm that is.

The Yellow Pages of your local telephone directory is another good place to obtain the names of temporary-help firms. Look under the heading "Employment Contractors—Temporary Help."

One other source of information is the National Association of Temporary Services (119 South Saint Asaph St., Alexandria, VA 22314). If you write and request it, the organization will send you a list of the names of the temporary-help firms in your state.

If you have friends who have worked for temporary-help companies, be sure to talk to them. Find out whether they recommend the companies they worked for. More people choose temporary-help firms on the basis of personal recommendation than for any other reason.

Determining Your Work Schedule

Before you present yourself at the temporary-help service for your interview, know exactly what days each week and the hours each day that you will be available for assignment. Of course, the greater your availability, the easier it will be for the service to place you. For example, if you tell the interviewer that you want to work every Monday through Friday from 9 A.M. to 5 P.M., then the chances are good you'll be given an assignment right away (if, of course, you are qualified). But if you tell the service you can work only

Wednesdays and Fridays from noon to 4:30 P.M., then there are going to be problems in placing you. This shouldn't imply, however, that you can't be choosy about which days and hours you want to work; you can. But it's important to realize that there is a direct relationship between your availability and the ease with which you can be placed.

If you prefer to work only a limited number of hours each week, it's best to schedule those hours over as few days as possible. Suppose you want to work only 20 hours a week. You'll get more assignments if you schedule those hours over three full days rather than over four or five days.

You will also be hired more readily if you are willing to accept jobs over a wide geographical area, which means you should be able to provide your own transportation or have access to dependable public transit.

Making Contact

To you, the job seeker, the temporary-help office you visit may look like an employment agency or a corporate personnel office. It may be located on the main street of a small town, in a suburban shopping center or in a high-rise office building in the downtown area of a major city. There may be only a handful of people applying for work or, if it's a large office, there may be dozens. Either way, things are likely to be a little hectic.

Try to plan your first visit early in the working day and early in the week. Many firms do not interview at all on Friday, particularly after noon.

Plan to spend about 90 minutes being interviewed and having your skills evaluated. At one of our offices, an applicant once rushed in and exclaimed, "Quick, give me the application form; I'm double-parked!" It's not quite that simple. Seeking employment at a temporary-personnel firm is very similar to applying for a full-time job with a blue-chip employer or an employment agency. It takes time.

Dress appropriately for a business office on the day of the interview; it helps to make a proper impression on the interviewer. Wearing blue jeans, a T-shirt and sneakers implies you aren't very serious about getting a job.

Be prompt. If you have an appointment for a certain time, it's a good idea to arrive a few minutes early. If you're driving, you should allow extra time for heavy traffic and parking.

When you arrive, a receptionist will greet you, then ask you to fill out what is called a "pre-employment application." Often the size of an index card, this asks you to list your name, address and telephone number, and also seeks to make a preliminary determination of your skills. From this list, you're asked to check those skills in which you have had work experience:

OFFICE	LIGHT INDUSTRIAL	OTHER
__ Clerical	__ Assembler	__ Cashier
__ Typist	__ Printed Circuit	__ Bank Teller
__ Transcribing	__ Machine Operator	__ Sales/Demo
__ Word Processing	__ Food Processor	__ Nurse
__ Secretarial	__ Packager	__ Technician
__ Data Input	__ Stock/Warehouse	__ Accounting
__ Bookkeeping	__ Order Picker	__ Engineering
__ Other	__ Other	__ Other

5

Call Today—Temp Tomorrow

Your capability is what's important in the temporary-help field. All the interviewer wants to know is: "What can you do?" "How well can you do it?"

Keep this in mind when you begin thinking about applying for a job as a temp. We realize that the idea of sitting across a desk from someone and asking that individual to hire you for pay can trigger all kinds of anxieties, a fear of rejection, a fear of failure. We know these fears to be very real. Indeed, a study conducted by the Yale School of Medicine revealed that 70 percent of women seeking jobs suffered from emotional strain, what the researchers termed "job hunter's stomach" and "interview insomnia."

But it's different in the temporary-help field. No one is going to reject you. Quite the opposite; what we look for is a basis for hiring you, that is, we seek to determine what skills you have and establish to what degree you've mastered them.

Don't be alarmed by the word *skill*. Everyone is skilled in some way. If you know the alphabet, can read, write legibly and perform simple arithmetic problems, you are skilled. If you can handle telephone calls, count money and make change and keep a checkbook balanced, you are skilled.

It doesn't matter when or where you happened to develop your skills—in school, through volunteer work or by virtue of some hobby or special interest. Maybe, as a young person, you learned to handle cash by having a newspaper route or running booths at church bazaars. That's fine.

The people you will meet at the temporary-help firm are specialists in the personnel field. They understand the thoughts and feelings of the job seeker. They realize that an older person may be ill at ease about her or his age. They can empathize with the retired person who is seeking to re-enter the job market and who seems bewildered by modern office equipment and the jargon of those who operate it. Interviewers expect applicants to be a bit nervous.

The mistake that some people make is attempting to mask their anxiety with an attitude of indifference, cockiness or superiority. Some applicants even appear hostile.

Avoid such attitudes. Be yourself. Keep cool. Tell us what kind of job you want. Tell us about your skills. We'll do the rest.

I'm certain that you will find the hiring process at the temporary-help service much more likely to produce fast results than if you happened to be seeking work at an employment agency or the personnel department of a big corporation. After all, the temp service is likely to have dozens upon dozens of jobs immediately available. Its client companies may be clamoring for workers. So everything runs smoothly, and the temp service interviews and evaluates you, sends you out on an assignment and then puts you on its payroll—and don't be surprised if it all happens within a couple of hours.

The Job Application Form

Before you're interviewed in depth, you'll be given an application or work-history form to fill out. Be very serious about it. The biggest single mistake that individuals make in applying for temporary jobs is their casual treatment of the application form. They fail to read it carefully, and don't answer the questions fully.

The application form is important for a couple of reasons. First of all, it gives the temporary-personnel firm the information it must have about your educational background and work experience to determine the specialized field in which you'll be working. And it provides the information that placement personnel require in pinpointing the appropriate assignments for you.

Look upon the application as an opportunity to demonstrate your value to the temp service. It gives you a chance to list your skills and accomplishments, as well as serving to demonstrate how clearly you can write and how well you can present important details. Read the entire form carefully before you start to fill it out. Take your time answering questions. Answer every question.

Be neat. An application that has a sloppy appearance may indicate to the interviewer that you are careless in your work habits. Use your best penmanship. If you don't write clearly, print.

If you make mistakes and have to cross out, don't hand the application in. Ask for another form and transfer the information from the first to the second.

If you do happen to have a resume, attach it to the application form. Don't leave blank any question that happens to be answered by the resume, writing "See resume" in the space. It's easy for the resume to get separated from the application form and become lost. Besides, the personnel specialists at the temp service want all the information about you in one place.

uniforce® temporary services

| TODAY'S DATE | / / |

| SKILL | 1 | Code | 2 | EMPLOYEE SOCIAL SECURITY NO. ☐ Verified |

Name (last) _____ First _____ MI ___

| U.S. Citizen Yes ☐ No ☐ | Do You Have Use of an Automobile Yes ☐ No ☐ |
| Alien I.D. No. _____ | |

Street Address _____

| Are You A Student YES ☐ NO ☐ | Have You Ever Worked For Uniforce YES ☐ NO ☐ | When ___ | Where ___ |

City _____ **State** _____ **Zip Code** _____

Have You Ever Worked For A Temporary Service? YES ☐ NO ☐   Which Ones ___

List Names & Address Of Firms Worked For As Temporary

1— _____
2— _____
3— _____

Room or Apt. No. ___ **Home Phone** ___ **Message Business Phone** ___

Why Are You Seeking Temporary Employment? _____

| Dates Available For Work | Circle Days Available | Day Hours | Night Hours |
| Start | Until | M T W T F S S | From To | From To |

☐ Will Accept Same Day Assignment?
☐ Available Long Term Assignment?

Are You Interested In A Permanent Position? ☐ YES ☐ NO

PLEASE ANSWER ALL QUESTIONS

Person To Notify In Case of Emergency	Phone	Address	City

EDUCATION (Circle Highest Grade Completed)

High School 1 2 3 4   College 1 2 3 4 5 6+   Degree or Major _____

Business or Vocational School _____   Other _____

PREVIOUS PERMANENT EMPLOYERS

DATES From	To	Name of Employer	Address	Phone No	Supervisor	Type of Work	Salary	Reason For Leaving

Have You Ever Been Bonded? — YES ☐ NO ☐
Have You Ever Been Refused A Bond? YES ☐ NO ☐
Do You Believe You Are Bondable Now? YES ☐ NO ☐

You might not be eligible for bonding if you have been previously convicted of a crime. Each case is individually considered

UNIFORCE is an Equal Opportunity Employer

How Were You Referred?

Newspaper ☐ Yes ☐ No   Which Paper _____   Which Ad _____   Friend ☐ Yes ☐ No   Name _____   Yellow Pages ☐ Yes ☐ No   Other _____

I authorize you and all former employers, given by me as references, to answer all questions and to give all information in connection with this application or in any way concerning me. I agree, if employed by you, that if I ever make claims against you for personal injuries, on your request I shall submit to examinations by physicians of your selection. My employment may be terminated by you at any time without liability to you except for wages as have been earned by me as of the date of such termination. I understand that if accepted for employment I will be working for Uniforce on its payroll, at its clients' premises. I understand that any information I learn while working for a client is to be kept confidential. It is agreed that I will obtain your permission before discussing permanent employment with a Uniforce Client.

I agree to immediately notify Uniforce at the conclusion of each assignment or as soon as I become available. If I fail to give such notice, Uniforce may assume that I am not available for reassignment, and am not ready, willing and able to work.

I state that the information provided in this Work History Card is true and complete. I understand that it shall be grounds for immediate dismissal if any of the information contained herein is found to be untrue. I will hold Uniforce harmless from any claims including, but not limited to, personal injury or illness as a result of my providing false or misleading information on this Work History Card.

SIGNATURE _____

Be sure to answer questions candidly. For instance, if there are any physical limitations in your ability to work, tell us about them. We must have this information. We do not want to send an individual with back problems on an assignment that demands that she or he remain standing for long periods.

Also be completely candid about your work history. We look for a consistent work record without any unexplained gaps between periods of employment. Tell us honestly why you left one job for another. Don't merely say "personal reasons."

Three or four good references should be sufficient. A good reference is someone who knows you and is familiar with your work experience. Be sure to notify each individual you plan to use as a reference. It won't do you any good if an interviewer calls one of your references and finds the person hardly knows your name.

Once you've completed filling out the application form, give it a final reading before handing it in.

Being Interviewed

The thought of being interviewed makes most people nervous. It's intimidating. For some people it's the illusion of the all powerful against the powerless. It gives one the feeling of being stripped.

When being interviewed for permanent employment, you are likely to be asked questions that sometimes are more probing. Typical questions of this type include: "What are your chief weaknesses?" "What are your long-range career goals?"

Forget all that. No interviewer at a temp service is ever going to ask you those kinds of questions. The temp-service interview is simply an exchange of information that is meant to determine what skills you have and how they can best be utilized.

Listen to the interviewer. Be sure to answer the question that is asked. Don't go off on a tangent. For example, when the interviewer asks you what days you can work, tell her or him exactly. Don't, as more than a few applicants do, explain in great detail the family involvements you might have. In other words, be professional.

Preparing for the Interview

The main thing to bring to the interview is your background and work-experience inventory (as explained in Chapter 3). It will enable you to have all of the information you need at your fingertips. If you have a resume, bring it along, but a resume is not a necessity. And don't forget to take your Social Security card, or, at least, the number.

Interview Tips

The majority of temporary-help firms evaluate all job applicants in four different categories: appearance, ability to communicate, attitude and job knowledge.

- *Appearance* Dress in a manner that is appropriate for a job you're seeking. If you're applying for clerical or secretarial work, dress for a business office. A woman should wear a skirt and blouse, or dress or suit; a man should wear dress trousers, a shirt, tie and jacket.

  If it's light industrial work you're seeking, you can wear jeans or other work clothes, as long as they're clean and neat.

  Your personnel coordinator will tell you when an assignment demands a particular dress code.

- *Ability to Communicate* During the interview, you'll be asked to explain in depth your employment background—where you have worked, exactly what type of work you've done and your reason for leaving any previous job. You'll be evaluated on your ability to communicate concerning these subjects. You'll be asked what type of work you want to do for the temp service.

  Be positive about yourself, your skills and your ability to do the job for which you're applying. Remember to speak clearly and distinctly.

- *Attitude* Be cooperative with the interviewer during the application process. You shouldn't show the slightest reluctance about filling out application forms or taking evaluation tests. If you do display a negative attitude, appearing bored or uncooperative, then the interviewer is likely to feel that's how you might act when sent on an assignment.

  Some people are nervous; they're not sure of themselves. They really don't know how to go about applying for a job. If this applies to you, just take things one step at a time, from the moment you enter the office and are welcomed until your evaluation tests are completed, and realize that all we're trying to do is pinpoint your skills and place you in a job in which you're going to feel comfortable.

  Other people display anxiety because they left their previous job under trying circumstances; they were fired. If you're in this category, explain the circumstances of your dismissal to the interviewer. Perhaps there was a personality conflict, or some other valid reason for what happened. In any event, it's not likely to be any stumbling block as far as the temporary-help service is concerned. Again, what's important to us is learning what skills you have and finding a spot where those skills can be used.

- *Job Knowledge* This has to do with your familiarity with all the duties and responsibilities that go along with the job you're seeking. If you intend to work as a secretary, for example, you should be prepared to explain what experience you've had in typing, taking dictation, filing, handling telephone calls, arranging conferences and meetings, reading and directing incoming mail, composing correspondence and carrying out the policies established by former employers.

Job knowledge is not only established during the interview but through various evaluation tests (Chapter 6).

Common Interview Questions

The information that interviewers seek does not vary much from one temp service to the next. Thus, the questions interviewers ask are fairly standard. The pages that follow give typical questions along with hints on how you should respond to each.

"Why do you want to work as a temp?"

The interviewer realizes that the chief reason you're seeking employment is likely to be financial— you need the money. Don't hesitate to state this, but also mention the secondary reasons. You can cite the convenience of temporary work, how well it is suited to your situation at home or to other responsibilities you may have.

You might answer that you're hoping your temporary job will provide you with work experience in a particular field. Another reason may be to simply alleviate boredom, to get out of the house for a few days a week or to meet new people.

"What kind of work are you seeking?"

Talk about your job skills in answering this question. If you're seeking work as a secretary, for example, cite your typing and steno speed.

Be as specific as you can in describing your skills. If you want to be a clerk, mention exactly what type of clerical work you've done in the past. Did it involve working with office files? With an adding machine? With a telephone console?

If the work you want to do is different from that indicated by your training and experience, be sure to make that clear to the interviewer. For instance, we have executive secretaries who ask for work as receptionists. They simply don't care to take on the responsibility that goes with being an executive secretary. And CRT operators sometimes want to work as telephone operators, or in some other job where their eyes will not get strained.

"What did you do on your previous job?"

Be as specific as you can in answering this question. Suppose you were a secretary for a CPA firm. The interviewer will want to know whether you worked for an individual or several persons. What were the titles of the individuals you worked for? Did you work for the financial administrator? For a vice president? The interviewer will also want to know what kind of typing you did. Did you type charts and statistics?

Even if you've had only limited work experience, don't hesitate to describe it; let the interviewer judge whether it is valuable or not. One of our applicants, in response to an interviewer's query, happened to mention that she worked in her neighborhood library on Saturdays as a clerk. She gave out the information reluctantly because she wasn't seeking library work.

However, by questioning her about the job, the interviewer learned the woman had gained experience in dealing with people, knew how to handle money and a cash drawer, could perform several clerical tasks and do light typing. The applicant was able to get assigned almost immediately chiefly because of the library experience she almost didn't mention.

"What kind of office machines or equipment have you worked with?"

Your skill in operating various office machines has an important bearing on the types of jobs you're going to be offered and how much you're going to be paid. Be as specific as you can in answering this question. Say, for example, "I've worked an IBM electronic typewriter, Model 100," or "I've used a Xerox memory typewriter, Model 620." Mention all word-processing equipment or data-processing equipment by name.

Also explain your experience with each machine. If you've worked with an IBM Selectric, what exactly can you do with it? Can you address envelopes? Have you worked as a copy typist? Can you handle statistical typing? How about billing?

Some machines can be described in general terms, without reference to the manufacturer or model number. Maybe you've handled a call director; perhaps you can operate a mimeograph machine, or the type of machine that collates automatically. The more machines you can operate, the greater your value.

If the interviewer asks if you are skilled in operating a specific piece of equipment and you haven't had experience in its use, mention what kind of similar machines you can operate.

"Why did you leave your last job?"

This can be a difficult question to answer. But if you were fired, say so. Be honest, and refrain from criticizing your former employer.

Maybe you were let go for economic reasons. "My whole department was laid off," you can say. "The company was cutting back."

Other reasons a person might leave a job include: it required too much travel; the salary was too low; it offered no opportunity for advancement; you decided you wanted to go into a different line of work; the company was reorganized and the position eliminated.

"Have you done any volunteer work?"

Give this question plenty of careful thought. Think of all the different types of organizations to which you may have belonged, civic or political, cultural or professional. The skills you developed in working with such organizations—writing, speaking, selling, organizing or supervising—can be extremely valuable. Don't fail to mention them.

"When are you available for work?"

When you're asked this question, be as specific as you can about the type of work schedule you can handle.

Can you work full days—from 9 A.M. to 5 P.M. or from 8 A.M. to 4 P.M.? That's the first thing the interviewer will want to know.

Can you work several weeks at a time? Sometimes jobs are available on a long-term basis: for example, five days a week for eight to twelve consecutive weeks. Would you be available to accept such an assignment?

Even if you are available to work five days a week, are you willing to accept short-term assignments? Are you willing to work a few days at one client company, then maybe a week at a second, and then several days at a third?

Of course, if you're available only on specific days of the week or only for certain hours on certain days, be sure to tell the interviewer.

The matter of transportation is likely to come up during this discussion, particularly if you're going to be working in a suburban context. The interviewer will want to know if you drive and have access to a car.

"Do you have any personal preferences regarding working conditions?"

Express any preference you have about your work environment. Do you have any objection to working in a factory office? What about air conditioning; is that important?

Some applicants tell us that they will work for only one supervisor, not several. Or an applicant will say, "I won't work for a woman." Another will declare, "I won't work for a man."

It's not uncommon for male applicants to request an office where there is a preponderance of single women, and female applicants have the same request regarding single men.

Naturally, every personal preference reduces the number of job openings available to you.

"Can we call references who are familiar with your work?"

Be prepared to give the interviewer the names and addresses of three or four former employers. Will the temp service check your references? Certainly. You'll be asked to sign a form that gives the company this authorization. Usually it is included as part of the job application form.

Your Rate of Pay

When the interview is over and you're offered a job, the interviewer will tell you how much you can expect to be paid. The amount is an hourly rate based upon your skills.

You'll be given a supply of time cards. (A sample card is pictured on pages 92–93.) You use a time card to record the number of hours you work each day for a full week. At the end of the week, the time card must be signed by your supervisor at the client company, thus certifying that the number of hours you worked is accurate and your work was satisfactory.

If you happen to be returning to the labor force after a long period of not working, you may not be familiar with current wage rates. To determine the approximate hourly rate for the job you're seeking, simply consult the classified advertising section of a local newspaper, and check the wages being paid to individuals whose skills are the same as yours.

6
Unleashing Your Talents

When you're being interviewed for a temporary job, you won't be wrong if you get the idea that the person conducting the interview doesn't care too much whether you happen to be female or male, old or young, married or single. Such matters as educational background and work experience don't seem to be too critical, either.

Temp jobs are task oriented. A client will call and say, "I need a good typist" or "Send us a good figure clerk." The client doesn't care about age or marital status, or whether the worker is a high-school dropout or a Rhodes scholar. She or he wants a person with specific skills. That's all.

That's why temp services put such an emphasis on skill evaluation. You must be ready to accept this idea. Not everyone is. "But I'm an *executive* secretary!" is one protest we hear. "But I have a college degree!" is another. Or sometimes a woman who is returning to work after a long layoff will say, "How can I take a typing test? I haven't touched a typewriter in 99 years."

People resist being evaluated because they have the idea that the tests are intended to serve as a basis of rejection. Not at all. They're meant to establish how skilled you are. If, for example, you're applying for a job as a typist, we have to know your typing speed. If you're going to be sent out on assignments as a file clerk, we want to know how fast and accurate you are.

Instead of taking exception to the idea of being evaluated, you should look upon the various tests as a means of documenting your marketability. Take as many different types of tests as you can. (They're described in this chapter.)

Suppose you're seeking work as a typist. It's important to establish your typing speed, of course, but also whether you have a speciality—manuscript typing or statistics, for example. Do you use transcription equipment? Do you take steno? Besides typing your own correspondence, are you capable of preparing it? Ask to take tests that will serve to establish your competency in any of these areas.

In addition, ask to be tested for any other jobs for which you feel you are qualified. A typist can also be assigned as a CRT operator, and vice versa. A file clerk can also be sent out as a telephone operator. The more jobs you are able to do, the easier it will be to place you.

Test Tips

When you're being tested, listen carefully to the instructions you're given. Be sure to ask questions if you do not understand exactly what you're expected to do. Remember, the time for questions is when the instructions are being given, not once the test has begun. Many tests have time limits. You'll be told how much time you have. Taking up precious seconds by asking questions can hurt your score.

Work steadily and carefully. While, generally speaking, it's better to be accurate than to be fast, don't spend too much time on any one question. Return to the difficult ones after you've completed the others.

If you fail to do well on a test, don't worry. Your initial score doesn't become a part of your record. Perhaps the equipment you used was unfamiliar to you. Find out whether you can use the equipment to practice. Then ask to retake the test.

Typing Tests

There are several different typing tests. If the typewriter you are to use for a test is a model or a brand that is unfamiliar to you, ask for paper and practice with the machine until you feel comfortable using it.

Every typist applicant is given a test on which she or he is asked to type two pages of typed material, line by line, while being timed. You have five minutes to complete the test. Should you finish before the signal to stop is given, you simply begin again.

Another test evaluates the applicant's ability to type a neat, well-arranged business letter. "The letter should be ready for mailing," the instructions say, "free of detectable errors and well balanced on the page.

"It is better to type accurately than to hurry and make mistakes."

The applicant is given a handwritten copy of a letter (see opposite page).

The applicant is told the letter is from Mr. Edward Floyd, Secretary Treasurer of Advertising for Personnel. "Type his name and title below the closing," say the instructions. "Leave sufficient space for his signature between the closing and his typewritten name."

The letter is to be addressed to: Mr. Henry R. Nor-

¶ Thank you for your letter enclosing the lease for our office at 3199 Walnut Street in Philadelphia.

¶ Would you please explain Paragraph 4 in Section II of the lease concerning the provision for air conditioning? We understand that the lessor ^that the lessee, furnishes ^the air conditioning.

¶ We would appreciate your expert advice.

¶ Sincerely yours,

———————————————

¶ = New Paragraph
^ = Insert

MEMORANDUM → Center by judgment

TO: Department Heads

DATE: → June 3, 1983

FROM: Lytton J. Ames, Comptroller

SUBJ: <u>NEW TRAVEL REGULATIONS</u>

(Set margins by judgment)

(As of this date) → All travel requests are to be made according to these instructions, which cancel those dated January 2, 1983 ~~for business trips~~. Please advise personnel in your department and have them initial this memorandum for your records.

1. ~~Arrangements for Business Trips~~ Transportation Reservations

Reservations for train, plane, bus, car rental *(or any other means of transportation)* should be requisitioned well in advance through the Travel Department only. If the cost of transportation will total $500 or more, obtain approval first from the Comptroller on Form 349A. Reservations are no longer to be made directly with the carrier. (If cash advance is needed, see Section 3.)

¶ A reservation may be ~~made~~ by telephone to the Travel Department, but confirmed on Travel Form 1045. Include complete details of the trip, it must be ~~be given~~, such as: date of departure, local arrival time, length of stay at each destination, and traveler's preference, if any, as to carrier and routing. Each item on the form should be carefully checked in order to avoid costly mistakes.

2. Hotel and Motel Reservations

Indicate the type of room desired. When a conference is to be held, reserve a function room if business. If arrival will be after 6 p.m., mark request, "Hold for late arrival," as hotels release unconfirmed reservations after that time. Request a confirmation. State people expected, whether or not refreshments will be served, and if so, number of, quantity, and kind.

3. Cash Advances

Request for a cash advance should be made on Form 268. For an amount over $1,000, the approval of the traveler's manager is required, unless the traveler is an officer. In that case, another corporate officer may give approval. The white form goes to the Accounting Department, the blue to the department manager, and the yellow is retained in the Traveler's own file.

ton, Vice President, the Norton Company, 630 Fifth Ave., New York, NY 10020. Instructions are given for style and spacing.

The test lasts five minutes. The applicant is instructed to type the letter accurately as many times as possible, proofreading each copy and correcting any errors.

In another typing test, the applicant is given a corrected and edited copy of an office memo (see preceding pages).

You must type a corrected copy of the memo. "Start and stop on signal," say the instructions. "If you make an error, correct it neatly during typing."

There is also a typing test to determine how fast and how accurately you can address envelopes. There's another test in which you are asked to type bills and invoices. Prospective statistical typists are evaluated by being asked to type statistical reports.

Secretarial Tests

Prospective secretaries are always given English grammar and spelling tests, in addition to typing and dictation tests. The grammar test (see below) asks the applicant to complete a series of sentences, circling the correct words in the columns at the right. "Do not write in the blank space in the sentence," say the directions. "Start and stop on signal. Your goal is accuracy."

Sample: A secretary usually _____ letters.   type   types

1. The new retirement plan does not _____ us.   affect   effect
2. He is a boy _____ we know can be trusted.   who   whom
3. The _____ problem is lack of space.   principle   principal

Unleashing Your Talents

4. I ———— hardly hear you with all   can   can't
the noise.
5. For an expert, ———— easy to figure   its   it's
taxes.

In the spelling test, two versions of each of fourteen words are listed, and the applicant is asked to circle the correct one. Here are some examples:

Sample:
stapling	stapeling
independent	independant
separate	seperate
managment	management
deductable	deductible
parallel	paralel

Stenography Test

If you're applying for a job as a stenographer, you'll be asked to take dictation from a specially prepared tape at your particular words-per-minute rate, then to transcribe your notes.

Clerical Tests

Individuals who are to be assigned as clerks are given a simple arithmetic test that involves addition, subtraction, multiplication and division. Here are some typical problems:

Addition	Subtraction	Multiplication	Division
5268	757,201	6259	7)2163
7729	−468,963	×897	
8653			
+4974			

You are also asked to solve problems such as these:

1. Of 460 employees in a company, 27 resigned and 8 retired; 11 new employees were hired. How many employees does the company now have?

2. You can move into a new apartment if you pay a 15 percent rent increase over the present rate of $125 a month. What would the new rent be?

Figure clerks are tested for their speed and accuracy in using an adding machine. They are asked to total several columns of figures. The following are typical:

11,001.10	62.31	7,028.92
15.75	25,689.75	126.62
18.00	56.79	9,999.99
20.25	(− 89.52)	(−1,485.96)
(− 123.75)	56.40	638.75
12.70	15,679.67	.29
139.25	(− 8,887.77)	(− .30)
8,975.63	(− 202.43)	222.52
.26	2,256.96	(− 222.25)
(− 3,525.72)	6,390.21	4,829.13

Each applicant is given five minutes to complete the test. If you complete the test before your time is up, check your work until you are told to stop.

A typical file-clerk test involves putting a random assortment of index cards, each bearing a different name, into proper order. The test instructions explain: "There are many basic filing principles," and then several principles are listed. These must be followed by the applicant as she or he files the cards. The principles include:

1. You cannot file abbreviated names. You must spell out abbreviations.

   Example: *File as:*
   U. S. Government   United States Government
   St. Vincent's Hospital Saint Vincent's Hospital

2. Ignore titles completely and file by last name first.

   Example: *File as:*
   Mr. Harry Smith   Smith, Harry
   Mrs. Mary Jones Brown   Brown, Mary Jones

3. Names starting with Mc or Mac are to be filed in front of the M's as a special alphabetized group.

   Example: *File as:*
   Donald McDermott   MacArthur, James
   James MacArthur   MacDonnell, Peter
   John McCann   McCann, John
   Peter MacDonnell   McDermott, Donald

After reading the instructions, the applicant is asked to file the cards. You are permitted to refer back to the instructions during the test.

Bookkeeping Tests

Prospective bookkeepers are also tested. Here are some sample questions from the assistant bookkeeper's test:

1. Indicate whether the accounts listed below would normally have a debit or credit balance:

	Debit	Credit
Cash	_____	_____
Accounts Payable	_____	_____
Selling Expense	_____	_____
Travel & Entertainment Expense	_____	_____
Sales Income	_____	_____
Notes Payable	_____	_____

2. Using the four books of entry listed below, indicate the letter of the proper book to be used for the following entries:

        A. Cash Disbursement
        B. Cash Receipt
        C. Purchase Journal
        D. Sales Journal

1. Purchase _____
2. Sales Invoice _____
3. Checks Received in Payment of Accounts Receivable _____
4. Checks Drawn in Payment of Accounts Payable _____

3. The accounts listed below have open balances as of December 31, 1970. Please extend and age each account.

Date of Sale	Account	Amount	Under 30 Days	30 to 60 Days	60 to 90 Days
Dec. 10, 1970	Mor Co.	$ 50.00			
Oct. 15, 1970	Hurst Co.	100.00			
Nov. 7, 1970	Cogland Co.	150.00			
June 10, 1970	Freckles, Inc.	170.00			
Dec. 27, 1970	Hill Assoc.	69.00			

Unleashing Your Talents

The applicant for employment as a full-charge bookkeeper will be asked questions such as the following:

1. Number the following accounts in the same order that you would ordinarily find them in the general ledger:

   Furniture & Fixtures   _____
   Accounts Receivable   _____
   Cash   _____
   Notes Payable   _____
   Capital Stock   _____

2. Gordon Robin's normal work week is 40 hours and his gross earnings are $200 per week. Gordon is to get time-and-a-half pay for overtime work. Using the figures stated below, compute his net take-home pay:

Hours Worked	50
Federal Withholding Tax	10%
State Withholding Tax	5%
City Withholding Tax	1%
Social Security Tax	5.2%

   (Net take-home pay)

3. Indicate whether the accounts below would normally have a debit or credit balance:

	Debit	Credit
Petty Cash	_____	_____
Federal Withholding Tax	_____	_____
Social Security Tax (Employer Share)	_____	_____
Accounts Payable	_____	_____
Advertising Expense	_____	_____
Sales Returns & Allowance	_____	_____

Re-evaluation

Bear in mind that the temporary-personnel firm looks upon any test you take as a measure of your present degree of skillfulness. It is no indication of how you might actually perform. After you've been working for a while, maybe for even as short a period as a week, your skills are likely to improve. Explain this to your personnel coordinator and ask to be re-tested. You'll find the temp service is just as interested as you are in documenting your improvement.

7

Becoming a Super Temp Is Easy

You may be offered a job on the spot during the interview at the temporary-help service. Or you may be called at home within the next day or so and offered an assignment.

It works like this: As soon as the temp service has a job request from a client company that matches your skills, a personnel coordinator will call you. She or he will tell you the type of job that's available, the name and address of the company, the name of the person to whom you are to report and your rate of pay. (There's space reserved at the top of the time card where you can jot down all this information.)

Then you'll be asked whether you want to accept the assignment. If you can, fine. But, remember, you can refuse *any* assignment. Maybe you're not feeling well, maybe you have made other plans for the day. Refusing an assignment now and then does not count against you. You'll be offered another as soon as one becomes available.

Be sure to ask questions if the personnel coordinator's instructions aren't clear. Ask for directions, if you're not sure of the quickest route to the company. Ask about parking facilities. Ask about lunch facilities. Ask about the dress code. Find out the name of the person to whom you'll be reporting.

Once you start working at the client company, keep in mind that your employer is still the temporary-personnel service. Even though a client-company supervisor tells you what your duties are and how to perform them, you are still responsible to the personnel coordinator at the temporary-help service.

On Assignment

Once you've accepted an assignment, you should do the job as well as you possibly can. You want to make a good impression, not only for yourself, but for your employer, the temp service.

Arriving on time is important in any job, but in the case of a temp assignment, it's doubly important. It is likely you have been assigned with a specific need in mind. If you're late, it could disrupt the flow of work for the entire office.

Plan to arrive 15 minutes ahead of time the first day. Allow yourself extra traveling time in case of heavy traffic.

Make a special effort to develop a smooth working relationship with your supervisor. When you arrive the first day, go directly to the supervisor and introduce yourself. Listen carefully to the supervisor's instructions concerning the job. If you have any questions concerning your duties, be sure to ask them.

If, for example, you have been assigned to work as a secretary, you might ask to see a sample of the client-company's letter format. Learn how to handle telephone calls. Do you announce your supervisor's name when you pick up the telephone, the name of the department or the firm's name? Is it company policy to ask callers to remain holding if the person they wish to talk with is on another call, or should you tell the caller that she or he will be called back?

If you're going to be doing any filing, find out which system to use—alphabetical, alpha-numerical or numerical. A temp who is going to be typing correspondence might ask whether she is to prepare rough drafts or finished copies of each letter.

The client-company's employees are likely to relate to you in much the same manner as you relate to them. Introduce yourself. Be friendly; don't be reluctant to smile.

You've been assigned to the company to do a specific job, maybe to help relieve a heavy workload. The regular employees may look upon you as a problem solver; they're ready to welcome you.

When regular employees are unfriendly or show resentment toward a temporary worker, it's usually because of a lack of communication; the company has failed to make it clear that the temp is merely a temp, that she or he is no threat to anyone's job.

Before you leave the client company at the end of an assignment, be sure to inform your supervisor of any work that you were unable to complete. Never leave a company without tying up all the loose ends.

Some temps complain that they are given menial or boring tasks when they are sent out on assignment, that they're handed work that no one else in the company wants to do.

The best solution to this problem is to learn new skills or upgrade the skills you now have. If you're sent out on an assignment as a legal secretary or a senior typist, it's not likely that the client company is going to place you in a dull and meaningless job. They can't afford to; your pay rate is so high that your supervisor has to make optimum use of your skills.

Becoming a Super Temp Is Easy

Occasionally, of course, every temporary employee gets assigned to a tedious job. When this happens to you, take heart in the fact that it's probably only going to last a short time. Tomorrow or the next day you may be moving on to work that is exciting or rewarding. You now have options!

What Not to Do

There are several things you should never do when on assignment. Don't make personal phone calls or conduct personal business. If you must make a personal call, ask permission.

Never open letters that are marked "Personal" or "Confidential."

Don't take extended breaks or lunch periods.

Don't give out your name and address when on assignment. If anyone at the client company wishes to get in touch with you, tell her or him to do so through your personnel coordinator at the temp service.

Don't discuss your rate of pay with anyone at the client company. You may be receiving more in hourly wages than some of the permanent employees. Should one of them learn of this, bad feelings could result. Your rate of pay is something you should discuss only with your personnel coordinator.

Last of all, don't discuss the work you've done with anyone outside of the client company. It may be of a confidential nature (even though this may not have been pointed out to you). Should a competitor learn what you have been doing, it could be harmful.

Keeping in Touch

Since you remain an employee of the temp service throughout the period you're on assignment, you should keep the service informed as to what's happening.

Call your personnel coordinator in any one of the following situations:

- When you are unable to report for an assignment because of illness or other reasons. Inform your coordinator as far in advance as possible.
- When you are delayed in getting to an assignment. Report this before 9 A.M., if possible.
- If you encounter any problems on an assignment—a job that is beyond your skills, for example, or a supervisor who seems unreasonable.
- When your availability changes, and you find you have more or fewer days to work.
- When you have any questions about your rate of pay.
- When your assignment ends. Are you then available to take another assignment? Your personnel coordinator will want to know.

How to Excel

When you are sent out on an assignment, the temp service *guarantees* you will do the work given to you by the client company. To do any less than your best could easily damage the relationship between the temp service and its client.

Your skills are only part of the story, however. A worker can sit at the typewriter and punch out copy at the rate of 90 words a minute, but her typing speed is meaningless if we give her an assignment and she's late in arriving or doesn't show up at all.

Reliability is one of the most important qualities you must have if you expect to become a super temp. Whenever you accept an assignment, the temp service is depending on you to be punctual in carrying it out, to observe the company dress code, respect client confidences and, all in all, complete the assignment quickly and efficiently.

Adaptability is another important quality. "It seems by the time I learn a job completely, it's over," said one woman about temping. It's a valid complaint.

Temping, by its nature, implies being thrust into a variety of job situations within a short span of time. You could work for as many as a half-dozen different supervisors in a period of four or five weeks, with each setting down a different set of work rules.

You have to learn to adjust to different types of people and different kinds of situations. You have to become flexible.

What else should you do to become an exceptional temp? We asked several veteran employees to answer that question for us. The following are some of their tips:

"Don't go out on an assignment with a preconceived notion of what you're going to do. Sometimes, for example, the company might not have your work ready when you arrive, so they'll give you a lot of other things to do. That's okay. It makes things interesting. But you should realize it's going to happen once in a while.

"You also have to be flexible as far as your coworkers are concerned. Sometimes you're made to feel that you're an outsider. The permanent employees don't make any effort to get to know you. It's like you're invisible or you don't exist. Why bother, they figure, you're only going to be there a couple of days. So you don't feel comfortable. But at other places they treat you like a savior. 'Sit down,' they tell you. 'Have some coffee. We're glad you're here. We need you.' You never know."

"Don't take assignments with the idea that you're

merely a fill-in, that you're going to do the least possible amount of work. Make up your mind to apply yourself. Have a willingness about taking on duties and responsibilities. You'll find your supervisors will respond in a positive way. They'll become more concerned about you. You'll be drawn into things. It affects your whole relationship with the company."

"Every business office has its own unwritten code of conduct. Some things are permissible; other things aren't. You learn by watching and listening, by not saying anything. It usually takes about three days to get the feel of a place. Just ease into things."

"Sometimes, through no fault of your own, you make people apprehensive, especially in an office where there is a lot of politics. When you show up the first day and start working efficiently, without having any problems, it can make the regular secretary fearful.

"So I make it a point on the first day of each assignment to let it be known that I'm not interested in a regular job, a full-time job. I don't mean that I march into my boss's office and tell him that. I tell my coworkers. I want them all to know that I'm not competition."

"Two people working in an office can usually have a good working relationship. But as soon as you add a third, you have politics. I watch what's happening, watch the maneuvering. But I don't get involved."

"Don't put up with anything that smacks of sexual harassment. I say this to young women especially, who aren't familiar with office procedures and who might feel intimidated by someone who represents the client. Call your personnel coordinator when you experience any sexual pressure and arrange to get another assignment.

"It happened to me once. One of the men in the office where I was working started getting fresh with me. I don't mind a little flirtation, but he made some suggestive remarks that made me feel uncomfortable. I called the temp service right away. I'd been temping for a couple of years and I had never made a claim like that before, so they were very sympathetic and arranged for another assignment for me right away.

"When the man who had bothered me heard that I had called the service and requested a transfer, he came over and apologized. 'I'm sorry if I was misunderstood,' he said. I felt that I had understood him perfectly."

"When I'm sent out on an assignment, I always take a few of my own 'tools'—some Ko-Rec-Type, a steno book and my own pencils. If the client company has supplies available, I'll use theirs, of course. But you never know what you're going to find."

"When you leave for work in the morning, assume the mentality of the job you're going to perform. If you're assigned as a secretary, then become a secretary in the way you think and act. It's like you're playing a role. What I mean is, leave your ego at home. It makes it a lot easier to fit into each new situation."

Traveling Temps

Once you have been hired by a temporary service, and demonstrate your reliability in carrying out assignments, you can work for that firm at any one of their offices in the United States. Suppose you've been working for Uniforce in New York, and you and your family are planning to move to Hartford or Kansas City, or maybe you're taking a vacation trip to Washington, D.C., or the Pacific Coast. Tell your personnel coordinator of your plans. If you wish, your records

ASSIGNMENT INFORMATION 28090 uniforce

COMPANY NAME _____

ADDRESS _____

REPORT TO _____ TIME _____

uniforce
temporary services

COMPANY NAME		WEEK ENDING SUNDAY
ADDRESS		CITY
JOB TITLE		JOB NUMBER
	SOCIAL SECURITY NO	

EMPLOYEE NAME

I hereby certify that the hours shown were worked by me during the week ending shown above, and were properly certified by an authorized representative of the named company at the bottom hereof. I understand I am to contact the Uniforce office after completing the assignment to determine if there is other work available for me. I agree that if I do not contact Uniforce upon completion of an assignment they can assume I am not available.

EMPLOYEE SIGNATURE

X _____

DAY	DATE	HOURS TO NEAREST ¼ HOUR			TOTAL HOURS
		START	FINISH	LESS LUNCH	
MON					

WED						
THUR						
FRI						
SAT						
SUN						

CUSTOMER PLEASE NOTE: ◆ TOTAL HRS. TO NEAREST QUARTER

FOUR (4) HOUR MINIMUM PER EMPLOYEE PER DAY

STRAIGHT TIME		OVERTIME	
HOURS	MINUTES	HOURS	MINUTES

CLIENT: BY YOUR SIGNATURE CUSTOMER CERTIFIES THAT: HOURS SHOWN ARE CORRECT; WORK WAS DONE SATISFACTORILY; AND THAT CUSTOMER AGREES TO THE TERMS AND CONDITIONS ON THE REVERSE SIDE OF THE CUSTOMER COPY.

CUSTOMER _____ DEPT _____

AUTHORIZED SIGNATURE _____ TITLE _____
X

IS THE EMPLOYEE CONTINUING THIS ASSIGNMENT? YES ☐ NO ☐

EQUAL OPPORTUNITY EMPLOYER MALE/FEMALE

UNIFORCE COPY

will be forwarded. After you've arrived and are ready to accept an assignment, call a personnel coordinator at the local Uniforce office. You should be able to get assigned immediately. There is no need to reapply or be retested.

Obviously, it's easier to get temp employment in some areas of the country than in others. In certain cities, temp offices are common and the business community is heavily dependent on temp workers. In other cities, temping is less important.

In which cities do temp services enjoy the highest usage? Here is a list (formulated by Donald Mayall and Kristin Nelson as part of a report prepared for the U.S. Department of Labor):

> San Jose
> Houston
> Anaheim
> Milwaukee
> Miami
> Tampa
> New York
> Los Angeles

Getting Paid

Getting paid for the work you've done is easy if you follow a few basic rules. At the end of each week, fill out a time card for each assignment you've had. Then have the time card signed by the supervisor at each client company. (Be sure to leave a signed copy of the card with the supervisor.)

Mail the card to the temp service or, if it's not inconvenient, drop it off. You'll receive your pay within a week.

Working Steadily

It's your responsibility to maintain contact with your personnel coordinator. Keep calling until you get the assignment you want at the time you want it.

It sometimes happens that an individual makes an excellent impression on the temp service, gets hired, but then is not placed right away. Why? It may be because the service is experiencing a slow period. Or it can also be that there is no client-company demand for the worker's particular skill.

If you've been hired by a temp service and you want to work more frequently than you are working, sign up with one or more additional services. Temp services realize that this may be necessary in order to keep steadily employed; they expect workers to do it.

If you do start working for a number of temporary services, be completely straightforward about accepting assignments. Don't cancel one to accept another. Take each as it comes.

8
You and Your Paycheck

All temporary-service firms make it a policy to periodically evaluate employee performance. After you have been assigned to a client company, your personnel coordinator will call your supervisor periodically to inquire about the quality of your work. Some temporary-service firms require written reports in addition to evaluations by telephone.

Rather than stand by and wait for your supervisor to file a positive report, you can help to make it happen. When you are complimented on your performance, ask your supervisor to pass on her or his remarks to the temporary service by filling out an evaluation form.

You can also ask your supervisor at the client company to write out a personal recommendation before you leave for a new assignment. Have it photocopied and distribute it to the personnel coordinators at the various temp services with whom you have registered. This tells the service that you are the type of competent person they want.

Poor Performance

When a personnel coordinator begins to receive unfavorable comments about an employee, the normal procedure is to investigate before taking any action. If the temp employee is found to be at fault, she or he is replaced at once. The next time the worker is given an assignment, her or his performance is carefully monitored. If an adverse report comes through a second time, the service isn't likely to try to place the worker again.

Sometimes the investigation shows that the employee is not at fault. The client company may have given the temporary service an inadequate description of the job, and the result is that the worker's skills are not well suited for the tasks involved. For instance, a secretary may be asked to take dictation that involves obscure technical terms; she or he is unable to do it. The client company should have specified in greater detail the *type* of secretary required for the job.

We have had clients who requested a "general clerk," and then asked the clerk to do some typing. If the clerk quickly proved to be a disaster as a typist, it's because the client failed to ask for a "clerk-typist."

Poor performance has also resulted from a lack of adequate supervision and direction on the part of the client company. The most efficient firms carefully plan the work the temp is to do, and some even prepare step-by-step instructions for the temp to follow.

Sometimes an employee is not able to perform well because working conditions are poor. Physical space may be inadequate. No one at the client company thought to order the extra supplies the temp needs.

I have to admit that the temporary service is occasionally the reason for poor performance. An interviewer may have done only a perfunctory job in evaluating a worker's skills, or a personnel coordinator may be guilty of carelessness in seeking to match the worker's skills with the job description. But such cases are very much the exception.

How to Get Higher Pay

The amount of money you receive is based on two things:
1. The type of job you're assigned to do.
2. Your skill in doing that job.

This means there are two ways in which you can maximize your rate of pay. You can strive to become a super temp (as outlined in the previous chapter). If you do an outstanding job on every assignment you're given, your pay rate will increase over a period of time.

You can also increase the amount you're paid by improving your skills.

Suppose the temp service for which you're employed sends you out on several assignments as a clerk-typist. One particular assignment lasts for several months. The hours fit perfectly into your schedule. You enjoy the job and you become very proficient in performing it. Your supervisor at the client company gives you more and more duties and responsibilities.

After six to nine months, you're undoubtedly entitled to an increase in pay. Get in touch with your personnel coordinator. Explain that you're doing an increased amount of work and have more responsibility than when you were first assigned.

If the personnel coordinator agrees that a raise is called for, she or he will contact the client company and ask that the firm approve an increase in the amount the temp service is billing for your services. Once approval is granted, the increase is passed on to you.

You can also earn an increase in pay by doing an outstanding job on every assignment you take. Once you feel you have proven your ability through a succession of good performances, call your personnel coordinator to discuss a raise.

Skill Upgrading

It's by improving their skills that most temp employees earn pay increases. Suppose you're hired by a temp service as a clerk-typist. Your typing speed is 35 to 40 words per minute. After several weeks of assignments, you become a better typist, increasing your speed to 45 to 50 words per minute. You should then call your personnel coordinator and ask to be re-evaluated. Once you've taken the typing test again, and it's been established that you type at the faster rate of speed, you'll automatically be granted higher pay.

This policy applies to virtually every skill area—to the secretary who improves her steno speed, to the receptionist who starts operating a telephone switchboard, to the clerk who goes from merely running an adding machine to performing bookkeeping functions.

You should keep on the alert for opportunities to acquire new skills whenever you're on assignment. As a typist, you may get some experience with a word processor. As a word processor, skilled in the use of Wang equipment, you may get introduced to the IBM Display Writer. In any such case, be sure to tell your personnel coordinator.

What all of this means is that you, as a temporary employee, never need to be satisfied to continue to work at a particular wage level. In the course of your assignments, you'll come upon countless opportunities to upgrade your skills or learn new ones, thus enhancing your value and adding to your earning power.

Opportunities in Word Processing

There are enormous opportunities today in the temp field for anyone capable of operating a word processor. Not only are temps required to replace the permanent word processors who happen to be on vacation or are ill, but they are also needed to step in when workloads go beyond the capabilities of permanent staffs. The demand for skilled people far outweighs the supply. You can almost write your own ticket.

This situation has skyrocketed the fees the word processor (the operator) is paid. Although it varies somewhat from one part of the country to another, the hourly rate is usually 40 to 50 percent higher than that of an executive secretary.

A word processor actually doesn't do anything more than a typist does, but she or he does it with far greater efficiency and speed. Like the typewriter, the word processor prints out pages of words. But it also does the job of a dictionary in spelling, what carbon paper or a photocopying machine does in making copies, what correction fluid or an eraser does in correcting errors, what a scissors does in cutting apart pages of text and what paste does in putting them back together again.

You do all of these things by simply pressing buttons. The machine turns out a perfect copy every time. And it's very fast. Some office managers say that the word processor is capable of increasing office production by as much as 200 percent.

In simple terms, a word processor is a machine that consists of a typewriter that is linked to a video screen and a word-storage system that consists of a tape or a disk. The "typewriter" of the word processor is divided into two parts—the keyboard and a printer. The printer produces letters on paper.

One important difference between a typewriter and a word processor is that when words are typed into a word processor the machine remembers what has been typed (somewhat like the way a pocket calculator remembers). You keep a permanent record of what you type by recording the words electronically on a tape or disk, a practice called "storing." Once stored, what you've typed can be recalled at any time.

The machine's video screen permits you to see what you have typed. It is also possible for you to retrieve and view any text that you've typed and stored previously.

Some of the operations of which the word processor is capable seem almost magical. Suppose you've just typed a two-page letter. After looking it over, your superior decides a paragraph must be added at the beginning. With a typewriter, that means laboriously retyping the entire letter. But with the word processor, you simply find the place on the screen where the paragraph is to be added, and "key in" the new material at that point. When you press a button, the new paragraph is instantly added and the succeeding paragraphs adjust themselves to its addition. Press another button and the revised version of the letter is instantly printed.

Or suppose after completing the typing of a letter, you find that you misspelled a word by omitting a letter. With a typewritten letter, you'd get out the correcting fluid, brush it over the word, then retype the word correctly, crowding in the missing letter. Or you'd retype the entire letter. With the word processor, all you have to do is find the word, indicate the letter you want added and where and press a button to key it in.

Some word processors have bult-in dictionaries that monitor your spelling. Suppose you frequently have trouble spelling the word *receive*. You can add receive to the list of many thousands of words in the machine's vocabulary, and every time you type the word, the word processor will see to it that it is spelled correctly.

The word processor is capable of performing many other chores. It allows you to transpose lines and paragraphs from one page to another, to select from a variety of type faces, to underline or print in italics or boldface or to send typed material from one desk to another or across the country. An author in the state of Washington, for example, used his word processor to send a book he was writing over telephone lines to his co-author in Colorado. The same author has established a data bank that knows all there is to know about what physicians and medical centers are getting the best results with which kinds of cancer treatment.

Word processors have transformed the way in which the modern office sends and distributes printed words—letters, memos and reports. An interoffice memo, for example, need no longer be distributed by mailroom clerks. Instead it can be sent through the office's electronic network and made to appear on the video screens at the various office work stations. No longer is there any need for long rows of filing cabinets crammed with folders containing copies of correspondence, memos or reports. Tapes and disks are stored nowadays.

Word processors are being used by companies of every type and size. Law firms, banks and insurance companies are among the largest users in the business world. Doctors and dentists use them. They can be made to store patients' medical records, fill out insurance reports and bill patients.

Retail businesses are reaping benefits from the

word processor, too. They can be used to keep payroll records, announce sales and send out reminders for payment.

Learning Word Processing

People representing almost every type of background have become skilled in the use of word processors. But before you sign up for a training course, you should be sure you are qualified to train. One important qualification is the typing skill. After all, the word-processing operator works at a keyboard that is almost identical to the keyboard of an electric typewriter.

Many personnel managers agree that the ability to type at a speed of at least 55 words per minute on an electric typewriter is vital before an individual embarks on word-processing training. If you can type faster than that, fine; you should excel in word processing. But if your speed is much less than 55 words per minute, you should take a typing course before beginning word-processing training. (Take the typing course at a school that offers training on a word processor.)

Another qualification is knowing the basics of spelling and grammar. Without this knowledge, you won't be able to check your work or edit dictation tapes.

You cannot learn word processing from an instruction manual or by means of a home-study course. You have to learn by using a particular word-processing system.

Chapter 11 of this book discusses where you can obtain word-processing training—through adult-education courses and proprietary schools and at community and junior colleges. The Association of Information Systems Professionals (1015 N. York Rd.,

Willow Grove, PA 19090) has prepared a "Directory to Information/Word Processing Education." It's free; write for a copy. Many temp services offer introductory training in word processing.

Choose the right machine to learn on. If you're a typist and skilled in using an IBM Selectric, you can also use a typewriter manufactured by Remington, Olivetti or anyone else, and with no drop in your speed or efficiency. But that's not true as far as word-processing equipment is concerned; there is no uniformity of operation. Just because you know how to work an IBM Display Writer doesn't mean you'll be able to run a Xerox 860; and because you know how to operate a Xerox 860 doesn't mean you'll know how to work a Wang word processor.

It's for this reason that you should train on the most popular make and model of word processor among business firms in your area. If you fail to do this, your appeal in the job market can be limited, even though you become very proficient.

Check the "Help Wanted" ads in your local newspaper to see what type of equipment is in use. Such ads are likely to mention word-processing equipment by brand name and model number. Talk to several temporary services in your community. Explain that you're planning to train in word processing and that you want to make the right decision as far as equipment is concerned. What word processors are the most popular? Also talk to word-processing operators. Ask what equipment they operate and whether there is a demand for their services.

Before you actually sign a contract, be sure to visit the school while classes are in session. You want to be sure the school stresses "hands-on" training. There should be an individual word-processing terminal for each student. Unless you can learn at a keyboard, your training is not likely to be adequate.

Becoming Permanent

Once you get hired by a temporary service and begin accepting assignments on a regular basis, and prove to be a productive and efficient worker, you could be offered a permanent job by a client company. Up to 30 percent of all temps are offered and accept permanent positions, according to statistics compiled by the National Association of Temporary Services.

Maybe such an offer is the fulfillment of your ambition; full-time employment was your goal from the outset. You became a temp and took assignments in an effort to build your confidence and at the same time appraise the job market. Now you've been offered a job you like. Congratulations!

But wait.

Before you quit as a temp and accept the permanent job, you owe it to the temporary service who is employing you to discuss the offer with them. Call your personnel coordinator and explain that you've received a job offer from the client company and you want to accept it. (It's likely the client company has already informed the temporary service that a job offer is going to be made to you.)

No temporary-help firm likes to lose an employee, especially with certain skilled workers in short supply in many parts of the country; no business does. Yet, as a general rule, temporary-help companies are willing to release to a client company any employee who has received an offer that she or he wants to accept.

There are, however, certain arrangements that must be made between the temporary service and the client company before the changeover can be completed. After all, the temporary-help service recruited you, tested you and perhaps even played a role in your training. The temporary service has an investment in you, and the client company will be asked to compensate the service for that investment.

This compensation can take one of two forms. The client company may be asked simply to keep you as a temporary employee for an additional period, usually 90 days, and to pay your regular wages during that time. As an alternative, the client company may be asked to pay a liquidated damage charge to the temporary service.

If you are offered a permanent job by a client company and you have no interest in it, decline the job offer courteously and promptly. Tell your supervisor at the client company that you appreciate the offer, but you simply want to remain working as a temp.

My advice to any temporary employee receiving a job offer from a client company is to think carefully about the benefits and drawbacks. Be wary about accepting the first offer you receive. Be sure you have a clear idea of the market value of your skills before you make a change.

Never forget the benefits you get as a temporary employee. There's the exposure you receive, the opportunity to meet many different kinds of people. There is no monotony in being a temp; going to work can be an adventure.

There are also the benefits you get in terms of skill development and personality enrichment. Don't cast these aside for what might seem like a comfortable niche without doing some serious thinking.

9
Temp Solutions

The number of women who want to work—and do—keeps spiraling upward. In 1960, according to the Bureau of Labor Statistics, women made up 38 percent of the labor force. It climbed to 43 percent in 1970 and to nearly 53 percent during the early 1980s.

The surging growth in the number of working women has affected every age group. In 1950, young women just out of school were the most likely to work. But by the 1960s, more and more women 45 years of age or older were joining the work force. These were often women with grown children who felt their responsibilities at home had lessened.

Temping often helps these women ease their way back to work. For example, when one of our interviewers perceives that a former secretary has some anxiety about going back to an office job after a long layoff, the interviewer is likely to suggest the woman take assignments as a clerk-typist or receptionist for a time. This gives the applicant a chance to practice her skills. She sees that the new office equipment is not nearly as formidable as she thought it was going to be. She picks up the jargon. Her confidence grows. After a few weeks, she's ready to resume work as a secretary.

"Returnees" still represent an important segment of the labor pool, but in recent years they have been joined by a growing number of married women in their twenties and thirties, including women with young children.

Most of these women work, not out of any great financial need, but simply because they want to enjoy a higher standard of living. "For the past two years, I've been making money working evenings and weekends as a temp, doing typing and word processing," says Beverly Campbell, 49, the mother of two married daughters. She and her husband, a civil engineer, live in the Philadelphia suburb of Jenkintown. "Last year I earned about $4,500," says Mrs. Campbell, "and I used the money to take my husband on a vacation to California. We do things like that with the extra money, things we normally couldn't afford to do."

Of the 40.5 million women who were employed at the start of the 1980s, it's safe to say that many of them were plagued with doubts and insecurities over their decision to enter the work force. It is not merely the process involved in getting a job—the interviews, filling out the forms and all of that—but the conflicts that arise out of being a woman during a time of enormous social change.

Most women are very tough on themselves. No matter which decision they make concerning their lives, they're distressed. If they have young children and work, they feel guilty. They keep thinking they should be home with the kids, or, at the very least, be there when they arrive home from school.

But if they decide to stay home with the children, they feel they're not being fair to themselves. They feel they should be able to develop careers and earn money.

These conflicts don't apply only to older women. A high percentage of recent college graduates grew up in homes where their mothers were housewives. They did not work outside the home. These young women have had no opportunity to learn from the work experience of others; they have had no role models.

How can you overcome the doubts and apprehensions that arise when you leave home to work? There is no easy solution. But temping can help. Temping can enable you to steer a middle course, to satisfy your husband and the children—and yourself.

Home and Family

It's a rare working mother who does not admit suffering moments of guilt as to whether her job and hours devoted to it are going to be harmful to her children. And the woman with grown children returning to the work force after a long absence is concerned how her employment will affect her relationship with her husband.

Initially, every working woman must come to the realization that it is simply not possible to continue to perform the same duties at home. Equally important, the husband and children have to realize this.

Changes and compromises have to be made. Other members of the family have to assume expanded roles in cooking, cleaning and running errands.

In the case of mothers with young children, temporary employment can ease the transition. These women can adjust their work schedules to dovetail with those of their baby sitters. A woman, for instance, who is able to arrange for child care only on Mondays, Wednesdays and Fridays, will tell her personnel coordinator to get assignments for her only on those days.

In an adaptation of that idea, a number of employees work in two-woman "teams." On Mondays and Wednesdays each week, one of the mothers stays at home caring for the children of both; the other takes a temp assignment. On Tuesdays and Thursdays, the two women reverse roles. What about Fridays? They're "normal" days.

Mothers of preschoolers who are not fortunate enough to have relatives or friends in the neighborhod often turn to day nurseries or child-care centers, which are usually administered by a city, county or state authority or by a private organization. Churches, YMCAs, women's organizations and various social agencies offer day-care facilities. As a general rule, these centers are operated in a professional manner. Fees are low to moderate.

The Administration for Children, Youth and Families (ACYF) of the Department of Health and Human Services has set guidelines a mother can follow in selecting a day-care center. She should establish that it is properly licensed, that the food is nourishing and well prepared, that there is room for the children to run and play, and the play equipment is sturdy and safe. The groups of children should be of an appropriate age range, and the staff should have a warm and friendly relationship with the youngsters. All in all, it should be a happy, comfortable, well-managed place for children to be.

Where the mother works is important to grade-school children. They're concerned about what would happen in the case of an emergency. It's a comfort for them to know the mother is close at hand, no more than ten minutes away. Temporary employment aids in this situation. When you apply for work, you can specify the area—even the neighborhood—in which you want to work.

The federal government, under certain conditions, will allow you to take tax credits of up to 30 percent of the amount paid for child care while you work or look for work. (Keep in mind that IRS rules are always subject to change.) To qualify, you must:

- File form 1040 or 1040A.
- Have income from work during the year.
- Keep up a home that you live in with one or more qualifying persons.

For more information, consult a local office of the Internal Revenue Service or obtain IRS Publication 503, "Child and Disabled Dependent Care."

The "Husband Problem"

When Mary Sullivan was in high school in Enfield, Connecticut, she wanted to become a nurse. But after graduation she got married, had three children in six and a half years and worked at home instead.

When her children had grown and she decided she wanted to go to work, she thought about becoming a nurse again. But she didn't feel like going to school for three or four years, and the cost, around $20,000, was much more than the family could afford.

Then her family doctor suggested she consider becoming a licensed practical nurse, an LPN. "It'll take you only about a year to get your license," he said, "and it's a lot like being a registered nurse."

It was good advice. After she investigated the field, Mary went to school, got her license, then signed up with a temp service in Hartford. "There's a tremendous demand for LPNs," she says. "I could work 24 hours a day, seven days a week, if I wanted to. But I usually only work three days. I don't want my husband to think that I've forsaken him completely."

Husbands, indeed, have to be considered. It wasn't

too many years ago that most married men cringed at the idea of having their wives take jobs outside the home. A married man prided himself on being able to support the family. If his wife worked, it was a sign of failure.

That kind of thinking has gone the way of pet rocks and skateboard parks. More than three-fifths of all married couples in the United States now have two incomes, significantly more than in earlier decades, according to Census Bureau statistics. As economists George Sternlieb and James Hughes noted in an article in *American Demographics,* commenting on the millions upon millions of wives that joined their husbands in the work force during the 1970s, "The good life in America increasingly requires a household economic team of two workers."

Husbands today usually react favorably to the fact that their wives are working. Home and family life improve. Not only is there added income, but the working woman enjoys the increased amount of social contact and feeling of greater self-reliance. She's a brighter and fresher personality, thanks to her new outside contacts.

Nevertheless, the idea that a "woman's place is in the home" has not perished. More than a few males feel that it is the role of the man to be the head of the household and the sole provider.

I never advise a woman to go to work if it is going to trigger family dissension. Temping, however, is something of a compromise in such situations.

One of our employees explained it to me this way: "My husband *said* he didn't care if I went back to work. But then he complained that the kids would suffer from my absence and that things would start falling apart around the house. 'Who's going to get dinner?' he wanted to know.

"Then I told him what I wanted to do was take a

temporary job, that I could arrange my schedule so I'd only be working two or three days a week.

"He liked that. His opposition melted."

The Age Issue

It used to be that job application forms contained a space where the applicant was asked to enter her or his birthdate. And during the interview, a question would arise to identify the applicant's age.

Such practices aren't legal anymore as they pertain to job applicants 40 to 70 years of age, due to the Equal Employment Opportunity legislation that grew out of Title VII of the Civil Rights Act of 1964, along with Executive Order 11246.

Such legislation was hardly necessary as far as the temporary-service industry was concerned. From the beginning, temp firms have had a reputation for hiring on the basis of individual merit. Period. Age has never mattered. One's race, color, religion, sex or nationality were never important in temping.

It's the same today. "Can you do the job?" That's the interviewer's major concern.

10
Crisis Temping

When 22-year-old John Robinson graduated from Haverford College in Philadelphia a couple of years ago, he and a classmate set out in John's battered Volkswagen with the idea of traveling around the United States for a while before settling down to their lifetime careers. It took them several months to make their way across the country. In October they arrived in Tucson, Arizona, where they planned to stay for a while.

"We were running out of money by that time," John recalls. "In fact, we were pretty desperate. We had enough money to put down a deposit on an apartment, but our food was running low."

Then John remembered that a friend back East had worked for Manpower one summer. They got the address of the local Manpower office from the telephone directory and paid a visit there one morning.

"We asked for jobs as laborers," John says. "We

didn't want to work in offices. We had just finished nine months of sitting in a classroom, and we were looking for something different. Besides, I prefer to work outdoors.

"Neither of us is particularly big or strong, but Manpower hired us right away. All we had to do was fill out application forms. We started getting two or three assignments a week. We did all kinds of things. We loaded automobile tires onto trailer trucks for a couple of days. One night we were assigned to install new racks and shelving in a sporting-goods store, move the merchandise into the store and have all the displays set up by 9 A.M. the next morning. Another time I got an assignment skimming the latex off of a big concrete pond at a plant that manufactured synthetic fibers. And on New Year's Eve, we moved a local lawyer's furniture and belongings out of one office and into another.

"Once the temp company found out that we were responsible people, that we showed up on time and weren't afraid to work, they gave us more and more assignments. They also liked us because we were willing to work any time of the day or night.

"We worked on and off for Manpower for the eight or nine months we spent in Tucson. My friend eventually got a permanent job through Manpower—as a roofer.

"I wouldn't like to work all my life as a temp. But at the time it helped us a great deal."

John Robinson's experience is one example of how temporary work can serve as a means of helping to alleviate personal financial pressure. Every segment of the work force feels this pressure, from those just entering the job market to newly retired women and men. This chapter explains how these problems manifest themselves and how temporary employment aids in solving them.

SUDDENLY UNEMPLOYED

Fired. Canned. Sacked. No matter which word is used to describe it, being dismissed from a job is never less than a wrenching experience.

Your first emotion is likely to be one of anxiety. Not only have your career plans been wrecked, the very basis of your life may suddenly be threatened. You start asking yourself questions such as, "How long are my savings going to hold out?" "What kind of sacrifices is my family going to have to start making?"

Your confidence is jarred, too. We live in a society where winning, becoming number one, is everything. Once you've been fired, you're not even in the game. You can begin to have serious misgivings about yourself, about your ability to provide for yourself and your family.

It's very normal to experience a period of emotional disorientation. What's important is how you react.

What you have to do is face up to the realities of the situation. Why were you fired? Was it lack of ability? Poor performance? A personality problem, your own or the boss's?

Try to give a rational perspective to what happened—and then move on. Work up a resume. Start looking for a new job. Maybe it's time to think about developing new skills. Or perhaps you want to consider a career in a different field. Now there is opportunity to do so. Whatever you decide, temping can help.

Emergency Income

Temping is one obvious way in which to relieve the financial pressure that accompanies being fired. While the temp job you get may not pay you as much as you've been accustomed to earning, it is a fast and dependable method of providing income when it's needed.

And you continue working as a temp for as long as the struggle to find a permanent job continues. "I had trouble finding the job I wanted in a reasonable amount of time, and I ran out of money," says a 34-year-old magazine editor, dismissed from her job when a new publisher took over. "I knew I would eventually find what I was looking for; I just needed more time. That's when I started taking temp assignments as a typist and proofreader.

"I didn't have any problem with doing temporary work, but some of my friends in the magazine field thought it was menial.

"There's nothing wrong with good honest work. Not having money—that's menial."

Another advantage of temping is that it gives you the flexibility of being able to go to interviews whenever they are scheduled. You can't afford to take a job that is going to hinder in any way your search for full-time employment.

Evaluating Career Alternatives

If, as a person who has been fired, you start dreaming about a different career, don't think it's unusual. Most people who are abruptly dismissed from their jobs go through periods in which they fantasize about taking a different type of job or embarking on a different career or profession.

Temping gives you a chance to put your fantasies to the test. It affords you the opportunity to look at a variety of different businesses from the inside. It's very possible to arrange a schedule that allows you to work in banking one week, publishing the next, advertising the week after and perhaps for a fund-raising organization during the week after that.

Once inside, you get to know a good deal about the company for which you're working, including the types of jobs that are available and the salaries being paid.

You also learn things about a company's personality. A woman temp had her suspicions of company sexism confirmed when she noticed that the office telephone directory she was given to use referred to males as "Mr. Davis" or "Mr. Taylor," while the females were listed as "Nancy" or "Debbie." Things like that don't ordinarily get revealed during a job interview.

Temporary to Permanent

The Uniforce files are bulging with cases of women and men who used temporary employment to snare permanent jobs. One of our secretaries had this experience: "One day the temp serivice called and asked me to take a one-day assignment. My first reaction was to refuse. I usually accept only long-term assignments, those that last two weeks or more. But my personnel coordinator pleaded with me. 'Please, please,' she said. 'This is our big chance with a new client. Please go.'

"So I went. I worked three days a week for a while, then two days a week. I stayed seven years."

One study of 206 temp employees found that 47 percent quit to accept permanent jobs. In another study, 48 percent of 149 employees gave up temping to take full-time positions. Both of these studies disclosed that as the workers became more and more skilled, the number of job offers they got increased, and their chances of remaining in temp work got slimmer and slimmer.

Chapter 8 discusses the pros and cons of taking a permanent job.

Other Benefits

Taking a temp job after you've been fired and while you're looking for full-time employment is a good way to keep your skills finely honed. If you're a secretary, for example, temping allows you to keep your typing and steno speeds at peak levels, maybe even improve them.

Your temping experience will also look good on your resume. When you're being interviewed for a permanent job, the interviewer notes that you haven't been merely sitting around and waiting for a job opening to occur. By going out and getting temp work, you stamp yourself as eager and ambitious.

And, remember, when you work for a temp service, your work history is kept on file. You can at any time ask your personnel coordinator for a written statement testifying to your character and ability.

Finally, temping can help you regain your confidence after the trauma of being fired. The daily challenges of the temp job and your ability to cope with them can't help but increase your feelings of self-esteem.

You're solving problems. You're achieving something. You begin to overcome those feelings of anxiety and reproach triggered by the firing experience.

Your mental attitude probably has more to do with getting the permanent job you want than any other factor. By helping to restore your optimism and develop positive feelings about yourself, temping has come to be regarded as a proven steppingstone to permanent employment.

MOONLIGHTING

Moonlighting, the practice of working an additional job, usually at night, used to be looked upon as an "economic phenomenon" by the U.S. Department of Labor, but there's nothing at all unusual about the practice nowadays. According to a recent study by the Department of Labor, approximately 4.7 million of the nation's workers hold two jobs, and the number is getting bigger all the time, growing at the same rate as the total work force.

The typical moonlighter used to be male, but in recent years more and more women have begun to take up the practice. Today about three of every ten moonlighters are women.

The second job, to which the moonlighter devotes from 15 to 20 hours a week, is not simply a means of providing a better standard of living; it's often an economic necessity. The moonlighter may have a mountain of bills to pay or one large debt, such as an automobile loan or a hospital bill.

Some moonlighters work at only certain times of the year. The wife or husband who takes a second job before the Christmas holiday is a case in point. Our temp offices across the country see an increased number of moonlighters just before April 15, when income taxes are due. People moonlight to help a son or daughter with college tuition payments.

There are also those who feel compelled to moonlight for psychological reasons. They're bored by their regular job or they may not feel appreciated. They seek a second job that will challenge them, satisfy them and at the same time provide extra income. "It's increased my self-esteem," says a clerical worker in the collections department of a computer manufacturer. "Now I know I can do two jobs. I have something I can fall back on should something happen to my regular job."

Analyzing Your Situation

If you haven't done any moonlighting before, proceed with caution. Do you have the stamina that working a second job demands? If there are any doubts in your mind, do only a modest amount of moonlighting at first, perhaps only four or five hours a couple of nights a week.

Once you have established that you are able to handle the second job, both physically and mentally, you can increase the hours you devote to it.

Also be sure to analyze how your full-time employer is going to react to the idea of your moonlighting. Some employers applaud workers who want to take a second job, feeling that it indicates the moonlighter is a person with drive and ambition, an individual who wants to get ahead. But other employers are put off by it. They feel every employee should give full attention to her or his regular job, that the woman or man who comes to work in the morning after toiling half the night isn't going to accomplish very much.

Be sure to discuss moonlighting with your employer. Assure the employer that your second job is not going to be detrimental in any way. Unless you have the blessing of your regular employer, your second job isn't likely to be worth your time or effort.

The Jobs

What kinds of moonlighting jobs are available? While there is a great diversity, most jobs involve clerical work, the operation of office machines, typing, word processing or data processing.

To some extent, the jobs for moonlighters are regional in nature. In an industrial area, there are frequently assembly-line jobs available.

Many of the moonlighting jobs we fill in the Northeast involve telephone sales or marketing. Moonlighting temps who go to work at 6 or 7 P.M. can place calls to people in their area as they arrive home from work and into the early evening.

To get a general idea of what the job opportunities are, simply think of the kinds of companies that operate on an around-the-clock basis. Such firms include not only manufacturing companies, but hotels and resorts, hospitals and health-care facilities, and some movie theaters and supermarkets.

When it comes to hours she or he wants to work, the moonlighter usually has several choices—from 4 P.M. to 10 P.M. (a favorite) or from 4 P.M. to midnight, or from 5 P.M. to 10 P.M. or midnight. Sometimes a manufacturing company, its production lines booming, requests temps for any one of the three eight-hour shifts—from midnight to 8 A.M., 8 A.M. to 4 P.M. or 4 P.M. to midnight. But an overwhelming majority of moonlighters want to work only partial shifts. After a full day at their regular jobs, four or five hours is all they feel they can handle.

The Future

The demand for moonlighters should remain strong in the years ahead—just so long as the nation's economy stays healthy. As the productivity of a company increases, management is faced with one of two choices: either to employ an increased number of daytime workers (which also means increasing the size of the plant or office), or employing a second shift of workers at night. Most companies prefer the second choice.

Productivity is one reason that hiring moonlighters makes sense. With the era of the electronic office, many jobs have become tedious in six- or seven-hour stretches. Entering data from checks into an electronic coding machine from 9:30 A.M. to 5 P.M. can be very boring. Many employees whose jobs are tied to a video-display terminal complain of eyestrain after several hours of work. Their productivity falls sharply at the end of the day. (This happens with all employees, not just CRT operators.) It doesn't make any sense to ask bored or fatigued employees to work overtime, so there is a growing tendency to rely on temporaries for second-shift work.

TEMPORARY JOBS FOR THE RETIRED

Kenneth Unger worked for 32 years for a tool and die company in Detroit. When he reached the mandatory retirement age of 65, he was made to trade his daily work routine and the camaraderie he enjoyed with his co-workers for a color television set the firm gave him and a twice-monthly pension check. He and his wife had seen their children marry and move away, and now they prepared to settle back and enjoy their "golden years."

"The first few months were hell, just plain hell," Mr. Unger says. "It was like I had a contagious disease or something. No one ever came to see us. The only people I talked to were my wife and once in a while the postman. A couple of times I went to the shop just to see how things were going, but the fellows looked at me like I was crazy. They wondered why I wasn't out fishing or bowling or something. I don't like to fish and don't like to bowl alone. I don't have real hobbies.

"I soon found out that too much time wasn't my only problem. Too little money was another. The pension was good and Social Security helped, but our income was still less than half of what we were used to. Then we got hit with some medical expenses that hurt, and we had to dip into our savings. To cut expenses, my wife started serving breakfast cereal for supper once or twice a week. That really stung. All my life I had been a good provider. Now I felt like a dud."

The Ungers eventually moved to California, where Mr. Unger went to work on a part-time basis for one of his sons, the head of a small electronics firm. Their problems—both psychological and financial—immediately eased.

Kenneth Unger is not an isolated example. Four out of five workers, willingly or not, are out of the labor market by the age of 65. As one specialist in the employment of the aged has put it, "It's really wrong to call it 'retirement.' It's unemployment due to age."

Like anyone who becomes unemployed, the retired person must withstand sharp blows to his psyche. The need to work—in this country, at least—is much more than economic. Working is what gives a person self-respect and a sense of worth. It provides companionship, serves as a source of pleasure and gives status. A person who retires is deprived of all these.

There's plenty of evidence to support this. The Midwest Council for Social Research recently conducted a survey of 6,300 older citizens in five Midwestern states that found: "The single factor most difficult in retirement was to have to give up working and knowing that you would no longer work. The second major difficulty, a consequence of the first, was having extra time on your hands and not knowing exactly what to do with it."

There's also the financial problem. The retired person usually has a pension and Social Security, and many states provide Old Age Assistance payments. Some receive financial help from relatives. But even though the retired worker may receive money from three or four different sources, in total it is often inadequate. Most mature people in the United States suffer a sharp decline in their standard of living.

A Retirement Alternative

Full-time employment is no solution for the retired worker. Most want a limit put on their physical activities. There's a disinclination to commute long distances, or to move to another city to find work.

There are also financial limitations, those imposed by the Social Security system.

Temporary work, on the other hand, offers retired women and men the opportunity to rejoin the labor force and resume meaningful employment. They're often able to utilize the skills they acquired in former jobs. There's no need to adhere to the rigors of an eight-hours-a-day, five-days-a-week work schedule. By temping, one can work fewer hours per day or a reduced number of days per week—or both.

And by keeping control of the number of hours one works, the retired person does not place Social Security or other benefits in jeopardy.

Building Social Security Credits

Many retired people, or those nearing retirement age, have come to realize that the income they receive as temporary employees can be used in accumulating the necessary "credit" required to maximize their Social Security benefits.

All temporary help firms provide Social Security coverage. They are required by law to do so.

To be eligible for benefits under the Social Security program, you must be credited with having performed a specific amount of work. Social Security credit is measured in terms of quarters of coverage. As of 1984, employees and self-employed individuals received one quarter of coverage for each $390 of annual earnings. (This amount will increase automatically in the future to keep pace with wage increases.) No more than four quarters of coverage can be earned in one year.

If you stop working before you have earned sufficient credits for coverage, you won't get any Social Security benefits. But the credit you may have already earned remains on your record. You can add to whatever credit you've accumulated by returning to work.

The following table shows how much credit is needed:

If you reach(ed) age 62 in:	Quarters of coverage needed:
1981	30 (7½ years)
1982	31 (7¾ years)
1983	32 (8 years)
1984	33 (8¼ years)
1985	34 (8½ years)
1986	35 (8¾ years)
1987	36 (9 years)
1988	37 (9¼ years)
1989	38 (9½ years)
1990	39 (9¾ years)
1991 (or later)	40 (10 years)

Suppose you are going to reach age 62 in 1987, and you've accumulated only 35¼ quarters of coverage. You need another ¾ in order to be eligible for retirement benefits.

The prospects of working full time are not likely to appeal to you. The solution is to sign up with a temporary-personnel service with the idea of earning $390 in each of three calendar quarters. To do so, you would have to earn an average of $30 a week for 13 weeks.

Even if you were paid the *minimum* wage and worked only two days a week, seven hours a day, you could accumulate between $500 and $600 in earnings in the 13-week period.

It's easy to find out the number of quarters of coverage you've been credited with through the years. Ask at your local Social Security office for the standard postcard mailer used in requesting a copy of your Social Security record. Complete the form, sign it, mail it and the information will be sent to you.

The exact amount of the benefits due you, or due your survivors in case of your death, can't be determined until you make an application for payment. But you can estimate the amount by following the instructions set down in various free publications available from the Social Security Administration. These include:

"Your Social Security"
"A Woman's Guide to Social Security"
"How Work Affects Your Social Security"
"Thinking About Retiring"
"How You Earn Social Security Credits"

To obtain any one or all of these booklets, write: Office of Public Inquiry, Social Security Administration, Department of Health and Human Services, 6401 Security Rd., Baltimore, MD. 20235.

You can also obtain more information at any Social Security office. There are approximately 1,300 of these. To find the address of the office nearest you, look in your local telephone directory under "Social Security Administration."

Social Security and Work

If you are retired but have decided you'd like to go back to work, and you have not yet reached 70 years of age, your earnings can serve to reduce the amount of your Social Security benefits.

You can receive *all* of your benefits, however, if your earnings do not exceed the annual exempt amount of wages established by the Social Security Administration. The annual exempt amount for 1984, for example, was $6,960 for people 65 to 70, and $5,160 for people under 65. (In future years, the annual exempt amount will increase automatically as wage levels rise.)

If your earnings should exceed the annual exempt amount, the Social Security Administration will withhold one dollar in benefits for every two dollars in earnings above the ceiling. Beginning in 1990, one dollar in benefits will be withheld for each three dollars in earnings.

It's obvious how temporary employment applies to this situation. Once employed by a temp service, you would work until you accrued the exempt amount of earnings for the year, then quit work until the next year.

For more information on wage exemptions, contact your local Social Security office.

TEMP YOUR WAY THROUGH COLLEGE

Temporary-help services are proving to be a tremendous boon to the college student seeking employment. Throughout the school year, hundreds of thousands of students register at temporary-personnel services across the country, requesting work assignments for the hours they're not in class or not occupied with studies. And during the Christmas holidays and spring break, students flood into temporary-help offices. The same is true during the summer months, which are among the busiest months of the year for the temp-service industry.

Tim Fox, a 19-year-old student at Rutgers University in New Brunswick, New Jersey, had this experience: "The summer after my sophomore year, I returned home to New York City and started looking for a job. It seemed like I was competing with a million other kids. When I went to the state employment service to check on their summer youth employment program, I had to wait three hours to see a counselor, and then I was told they had no job leads.

"I read newspaper ads and checked out the neighborhood supermarket and some other stores. Nothing. Even though I needed money from a job to help pay my college expenses, I started thinking about doing volunteer work at a hospital. At least it would look good on my resume.

"Then a relative of mine told me about temping. I had heard of it, but only had a vague idea of what it was. I looked in the Yellow Pages of the Manhattan telephone book, and there were seven pages of listings for temp-help companies. I think half of the offices on 42nd Street between Fifth and Lexington Avenues were temp offices. I picked out one at random one afternoon and dropped in. They gave me an application form to fill out and then I took some tests. Afterward they told me they could get me work as a clerk, which sounded fine. A couple of days later, the service called and offered me a clerical job with a clothing manufacturer. I spent the next three days sorting garment hangtags, putting them in batches. I worked with two other temps. One of them told me that if I wanted to work a lot that I should sign up with two or three other temp services—so I did.

"Soon I was working four and five days a week, or as much as I wanted to. It seemed strange. A few weeks before, no one was even interested in talking to me about a job, and now I had companies competing for my 'talents.' It was terrific."

We can't say that Tim's experience is exactly typical, and we can't promise that temp services are going to vie with one another to employ you. But we can say that college students are being utilized by temp services in every part of the country.

We admire students for their intelligence and vitality—and for the skills they have. Most are skilled as typists and know how to use calculators. They can be quickly trained to use CRT equipment; more and more of them know how to operate word processors.

Besides the clerical jobs to which they get assigned, we place many college temps in retail outlets as salespersons during holiday periods. They also wrap, pack, ticket and stock shelves. Some college women get jobs demonstrating cosmetics at holiday time.

Getting Hired

When you're interviewed by the temp service, you'll be asked what subjects you're majoring in, and from your answers the interviewer will be able to get an idea of the type of work for which you're qualified. For example, an accounting major is likely to have had experience with a calculator and can do figure work. Marketing majors, we've found, are often well suited for telephone survey work or assignments as sales demonstrators.

History majors, or English majors, or other students without training in a skill area, are frequently assigned clerical jobs. They usually know how to type (even if they're not going to win any contests for speed). They know how to run adding machines. They can file and do record keeping.

The extracurricular activities in which you're involved can be important. Perhaps you're working for a campus newspaper or radio station, in which case you may be able to be placed in a job where organization, interpretation and communication are important.

Even if your activities don't *appear* to be job related, mention them anyway. Serving as the captain of a sports team, for example, shows you have leadership ability. Handling props for a theater group indicates your organizational skill.

Job Benefits

Temporary-work assignments are not merely important for the income they provide. They are also learning experiences for the student. An accounting major may tell us, for example, it is valuable simply to see how the accounting department of a big company functions, get an idea of what the atmosphere is like.

Temporary-work assignments have another value. As you near graduation, make a career choice and start seeking employment, you suddenly realize that business firms are extremely interested in your work history, however slight it may be. Personnel directors want to know, first of all, whether you worked and, if you did, they want to know in specific terms the type of work you performed. In other words, temporary work can do a great deal toward enhancing your resume.

Oftentimes a student will develop such a good working relationship with a client company that the firm will ask to have the student return during the next vacation break or even for the summer. Or sometimes students develop a fondness for a particular company, or a particular department of a company. They ask to be assigned to that company or department whenever an opening develops.

Almost every temp firm can report countless instances of students whose vacation assignments led to full-time positions after graduation.

A Foot in the Door

This suggests another use to which temp employment is being put. More and more newly graduated college students are using temping as means of gaining access to the professional world. Take the case of 22-year-old Susan Waggoner, who arrived in New York City several years ago with a brand-new degree from the University of Iowa and the ambition to launch a career in book publishing. She had no work experience worth mentioning. She had no marketable skills. "I didn't even know how to type," she says.

Friends of Susan who were actors, and who worked for temp agencies between roles, told her about Career Blazers, a temp service that specializes in placing people in the publishing field. Susan made an appointment with the service, was interviewed and hired.

"I really didn't have too much of a choice," she recalls. "I needed money desperately. I couldn't afford the luxury of spending the time looking for a full-time job.

"The service kept me busy. I worked five days a week, full time. I not only worked at the bigger houses, but also at some of the smaller specialized publishing companies.

"I passed the typing test at Career Blazers, which enabled me to get assignments as a typist rather than as a clerk. Even so, I wasn't making much money; waiting tables would have been more lucrative. But temping gave me a chance to get inside publishing and look around.

"I found that I enjoyed working more at a medium-sized publishing house than at a large company. I met a variety of people there. I got to know the entire operation. With a big company you can get stuck in one department and get lost.

"After I had been working as a temp for three or four months, I began to get offers of permanent jobs. I accepted one of these, becoming an editorial assistant at a medium-sized company. That was in December. I had started working for the temp service the previous May.

"I stayed with that company for about a year—or until I came to realize that I didn't like working in book publishing. I left and went back to work as a temp for a while, and later I started free-lance writing. That's what I'm doing today."

Susan Waggoner used temping as an entree. "It helps you to get to know the system," she says.

Realize, of course, you're not going to begin at the top of the heap. I say this because a minority of students feel that clerical or secretarial work is beneath them. They're seeking to break in at the executive level. That's not going to happen, of course. There are no shortcuts.

What a temp job does is provide an opportunity. It gets you inside. Then it's up to you to open the doors.

11
Maximizing Your Options

Several years ago when public-school teachers in New York City were on strike for more than two months, they crowded into the city's temporary-help offices seeking employment. That experience taught the teachers something. Thousands were dismayed to find that their college training and classroom experience did not have great value when it came to getting work.

While the temp services were able to find employment for those who had degrees in accounting or bookkeeping, or those who had been teaching typing or steno, and hundreds were placed in clerical jobs, many teachers never found work.

This episode pointed up how much better it is to be skilled. The temporary-personnel field deals largely in task-oriented jobs. Of course, we find employment for unskilled workers in the clerical and light industrial fields, but possessing a finely honed skill maximizes your options. You find you're in demand in the job marketplace. You can be selective.

In other words, being skilled puts you in control. It also imparts a feeling of assurance and optimism.

The need to be skilled is getting more acute all the time. Recent years have seen the development of the electronic office, in which many tasks are performed by computers and other machines representing new technologies. This trend is gathering force. In 1984, there were about 12.7 million video-display terminals, personal computers, word processors and the like in use in the United States, according to the International Data Corporation, a market-research firm in Framingham, Massachusetts. That number is expected to rise to 41 million before the end of the decade.

Every business office and industrial plant has been touched by the computer revolution. Virtually every job category has been affected. The best evidence of this is the "Help Wanted" section of your local newspaper. It is likely to offer dozens of different jobs that weren't even known a decade ago. And these are jobs that require skilled people.

Fortunately, there is no reason an individual has to be designated as unskilled nowadays. Business and industry, private educational organizations, and local, state and federal governments all offer training and retraining programs that cover every conceivable skill area. You can study part time or full time. You can study in a classroom, on the job or at home. Costs are generally very modest; sometimes instruction is free. All you really need to do is take the first step.

Temporary-Personnel Services

The offices of most temporary-personnel companies will help you become skilled or improve your skills by providing a variety of office machines—chiefly typewriters and adding machines—on which you can practice. Some offer well-planned, fully developed courses to teach office skills.

During the early 1980s, when an acute demand for

word processors developed, many temp firms offered training in word processing. A leading temporary service, for example, developed an innovative training program that used a diskette system and the word processor itself in which the machine actually "spoke" to the trainee, guiding her or him through each step of its operation.

That company offered word-processing training on four different levels:

1. *Entry Training*   For the clerical worker who had basic typing skills (40 wpm) and wanted to develop another marketable skill.

2. *Basic Training*   For the word-processing operator who had some hands-on experience and wanted to upgrade her or his level of word-processing skill, or for the operator returning to the work force who was seeking a brush-up course.

3. *Cross Training*   For an experienced operator who wanted to learn to use a second or third type of word processor.

4. *Advanced-Skill Training*   For operators who had mastered basic functions of the word processor through on-the-job experiences and wished to become skilled in use of the machine for statistical or mathematical functions.

Other major temporary services also offered word-processing training.

Such courses, however, are no substitute for classroom instruction and work experience in word processing. Most experts agree that at least 40 classroom hours are necessary merely to get an idea of what the machine can do.

Besides classroom training, it takes plenty of hands-on experience to become skilled. You must expect to spend from six to twelve months as an office word processor before you can expect to be qualified to receive top pay rates.

Public School Adult Education

No matter where you live—in a large city, a small town or in the suburbs—the best way to learn new job skills or improve the skills you now have is through an adult-education program offered by your local public school system. In the United States, about 21 million people are participating in adult education.

Women and men find that adult-education courses are a comfortable way to learn. The classes are usually held at night in the same classrooms used by children during the day. Tuition fees are low. Your classmates are your friends and neighbors.

Adult education took a big step forward with the Manpower Development and Training Act of 1962 and the Economic Opportunity Act of 1964. These furnished funds to train unemployed adults and also established the Adult Basic Education Program.

More change came in 1970 when many schools became community schools, and dedicated themselves to serving the entire community—adults as well as children. Another trend had to do with recurrent education, which is meant to help adults keep up with new developments in their businesses or professions.

There is a growing awareness today that a high-school diploma or college degree no longer signals a person's education has ended. Learning is a lifetime activity.

To find out about adult-education programs in your area, simply call your local high school, trade school or board of education.

Also consult the Yellow Pages of your telephone directory. Look for an "Adult Education" listing under the "Schools" heading.

Proprietary Schools

Proprietary schools include private business colleges, technical institutes and trade schools. There are about 1,300 such schools in the United States with an enrollment of 600,000.

Most proprietary schools teach vocational skills for accountants, typists, bookkeepers, stenographers and computer operators. In New York City alone, there are 19 such schools that offer word-processing courses.

Consult the Yellow Pages of your local telephone directory for the names of proprietary schools, for the "School Guide" under the "Schools" heading.

Some states require schools to be licensed or at least "approved." In any case, investigate any school in which you plan to enroll. Speak to students, graduates and employers. Also query the local office of the Better Business Bureau. Don't sign up without visiting the school to determine whether the classes are small and the environment comfortable.

Community Colleges, Junior Colleges

There are about 700 community colleges and junior colleges throughout the country, with virtually all of them offering advanced training in word processing, data processing, secretarial science, health services, banking and countless other semiprofessional and technical fields. Students learn skills for such jobs as computer operator, word processor, secretary, accountant, laboratory assistant and medical assistant.

Community colleges and junior colleges are invariably two-year colleges that allow students to enroll on a part-time basis. Evening classes as well as daytime classes are scheduled. Since many of these colleges receive funds from local or state governments, tuition fees are usually much lower than four-year institutions.

Extension Services

The extension service is a type of adult education that many universities offer in addition to their regular programs. It usually stresses technical training and courses to help professionals keep up with developments in their fields.

Such courses are normally intended for students who are unable to attend the university proper, usually because they live a good distance from the campus, so the campus, in effect, comes to them; it "extends" itself. An extension-service student might study by mail, attend extension classes organized in her or his community or listen to lecturers sent out by the school.

Extension services are a feature of colleges and universities in every state. They are almost certain to be offered in your community.

Home-Study Schools

The home-study school is an institution that furnishes educational material through the mail. There are about 3 million persons enrolled in the more than 500 home-study schools in the United States. About 75 percent of the courses are vocational in nature, that is, they offer instruction in an occupation or profession.

Colleges and universities are in the forefront of home-study education, providing correspondence courses for nearly 400,000 persons. Government agencies, the armed forces, religious institutions and business and industry furnish courses to over 1.7 million persons. Another 1.5 million persons are enrolled in private home-study schools.

It doesn't matter whether you sign up with a college or university, or enroll with a private institution; the quality of the instructional material you receive is almost certain to be first class. Textbooks are prepared with greater clarity and visual appeal today than in the past. There is a greater emphasis on getting you to understand and assimilate what's written. Often a course will be offered by means of an elaborate instruction kit, not merely a textbook and a lesson plan.

There are many advantages in signing up for a home-study course. You don't have to travel to and from a classroom. You can study at a time that is convenient; you never have to take time off from your job; you never have to leave your family. And home instruction generally costs less than classroom instruction.

Another benefit is that you set your own pace, advancing as fast as you like through those portions of the course that offer no problem, lingering whenever things get difficult.

But this advantage suggests a disadvantage. Since no instructor is impelling you to keep to a fixed schedule, it's easy to postpone a work period or an assignment. Ambition wanes; goals somehow diminish in importance. Unless you have the ability to work independently, choose some other method of instruction. Correspondence courses have an extremely high dropout rate.

Of course, not all subjects lend themselves to home study. Computer programming or word processing, subjects that require hands-on training, are two that should be taught by a qualified instructor. Nevertheless, there is a rich variety available. For instance, LaSalle Extension University (417 South Dearborn St., Chicago, IL 60605), a leader in home instruction, offers courses in accounting, bookkeeping, business law and typing. The school also offers courses for anyone wishing to become a dental assistant, secretary or stenographer. Write to LaSalle and ask for a free catalog.

You might also wish to write to the National Home Study Council (1601 Eighteenth St., N.W. Washington, DC 20009) for a free copy of the "Directory of Accredited Private Home-Study Schools." This is a listing of the more than 500 schools that make up the council's membership along with a rundown of the courses offered by each. Remember to enclose a self-addressed, No. 10-size stamped envelope.

Instruction Books

Self-teaching courses in the form of instruction books and manuals are available at your local public library or bookstore. Many of these are similar in form and content to correspondence courses, and thus have many of the same advantages and disadvantages.

The following list is a sampling of what's available:

Career Guide for Word Processing
By Hal Cornelius and William Lewis
Monarch Press, 1983
Division of Simon and Schuster
1230 Avenue of the Americas
New York, NY 10020
$7.95

Word Processing Concepts and Careers
By Marty Bergerud and Jean Gonzalez
John Wiley & Sons, 1981 (Second Edition)
605 Third Avenue
New York, NY 10158
$16.95

Quick Typing: A Self-Teaching Guide
By Jeremy Grossman

John Wiley & Sons, 1980
605 Third Avenue
New York, NY 10158
$5.95

Typing for Beginners
By Betty Owen
Perigee Books, 1976
c/o G. P. Putnam's
200 Madison Avenue
New York, NY 10016
$3.95

Quickscript; The Fast & Simple Shorthand Method
By Adele Booth Blanchard
Arco Publishing Co., 1982
215 Park Avenue South
New York, NY 10016
$5.95

Clear and Simple Shorthand
By Silas M. Wesley
Julian Messner Books, 1983 (Third Edition)
Division of Simon and Schuster
1230 Avenue of the Americas
New York, NY 10020
$7.95

Instructor's Book for Gregg Shorthand
By John R. Gregg, Louis A. Leslie,
  and Charles E. Zoubek
Gregg Division, McGraw-Hill Book Co., 1978
1221 Avenue of the Americas
New York, NY 10020
$7.50

Practical Guide to Bookkeeping and Accounting
By Ralph Fallig
Grosset & Dunlap, 1982
200 Madison Ave.

New York, NY 10016
$3.95

Office Machines, A Practical Approach
By Jimmy C. McKenzie and Robert J. Hughes
William C. Brown Publishing Co., 1983 (Second Edition)
2400 Kerper Blvd.
Dubuque, IA 52001
$16.95

Federally Aided Programs

High unemployment during the 1960s and 1970s prompted the federal government to establish a vast assortment of vocational training programs for men and women. Indeed, there are so many different federally aided programs now available it is not difficult to become bewildered by them.

The Manpower Development and Training Act of 1962 provided federal funds to train unemployed adults. The Vocational Education Act of 1963 furnished money for new buildings, programs and teacher training. The Economic Opportunity Act of 1964 brought the Job Corps into being. A law called the Vocational Education Amendments of 1968 expanded training opportunities for the handicapped and disadvantaged. The Comprehensive Employment and Training Act of 1973, called CETA, provided federal money to state and local governments for vocational education. The Education Amendments of 1976 provided funds to help overcome sex bias in vocational education.

Some 15 different federal bureaus and agencies administer these programs. For information about one or more of them, begin with a call to a local office of your state's education or labor departments. If you should happen to live in a metropolitan area, get in touch with the local office of the Department of Education.

The U.S. Department of Labor helps to provide training for persons who want to become skilled craftspersons under the provisions of a nationwide apprenticeship program. The department seeks to enlist the cooperation of both management and labor in the development of courses that provide on-the-job experience and related instruction, with the trainee recognized as an employed worker. For more information about the apprenticeship program, as well as a list of apprenticeable occupations, write for a free copy of "The National Apprenticeship Program," addressing your request to the U.S. Department of Labor, Manpower Administration, Washington, DC 20210

On October 1, 1983, many of the responsibilities for job training that had traditionally been carried out by the federal government were handed over to state and local governments under the terms of the Job Training Partnership Act. In addition, a public/private partnership came into existence that was intended to plan and design training programs and deliver training services.

For information about the Job Training Partnership program in your area, contact a Federal Job Information Center. These operate on a regional basis in the cities listed below. You can get information by mail, telephone, or on an in-person basis.

FEDERAL JOB INFORMATION CENTERS

ALABAMA
  Huntsville:
    Southerland Building
    808 Governors Drive, S.W. 35801
    (205) 453-5070

Maximizing Your Options

ALASKA

Anchorage:
Federal Building
701 C Street 99513
(907) 271-5821

ARIZONA

Phoenix:
522 N. Central Avenue 85004
(602) 261-4736

ARKANSAS

Little Rock:
Federal Building, Room 3421
700 W. Capitol Avenue 72201
(501) 378-5842

CALIFORNIA

Los Angeles:
Linder Building
845 S. Figueroa 90017
(213) 688-3360

Sacramento:
1029 J Street, Room 202
(916) 440-3441

San Diego:
880 Front Street 92188
(714) 293-6165

San Francisco:
Federal Building, Room 1001
450 Golden Avenue 94102
(415) 556-6667

COLORADO

Denver:
1845 Sherman Street 80203
(303) 837-3509

CONNECTICUT

Hartford:
Federal Building, Room 717
450 Main Street 06103
(203) 244-3096

DELAWARE

Wilmington:
Federal Building
844 King Street 19801
(302) 573-6288

DISTRICT OF COLUMBIA

Metro Area:
1900 E Street, N.W. 20415
(202) 737-9616

FLORIDA

Orlando:
80 N. Hughey Avenue 32801
(306) 420-6148

GEORGIA

Atlanta:
Richard B. Russell Federal Building
75 Spring Street, S.W. 30303
(404) 221-4315

HAWAII

Honolulu:
Federal Building, Room 1310
300 Ala Moana Boulevard 96850
(808) 546-7108

ILLINOIS

Chicago:
Dirksen Building, Room 1322
219 S. Dearborn Street 60604
(312) 353-5136

INDIANA

Indianapolis:
46 E. Ohio Street, Room 123, 46204
(317) 269-7161

IOWA

Des Moines:
210 Walnut Street, Room 191, 50309
(515) 284-4546

KANSAS

Wichita:
One-Twenty Building, Room 101
120 S. Market Street 67202
(316) 269-6106

LOUISIANA

New Orleans:
F. Edward Hebert Building
610 South Street, Room 103, 70130
(504) 589-2763

MARYLAND

Baltimore:
Garmatz Federal Building
101 W. Lombard Street 21201
(301) 962-3822

DC Metro Area:
1900 E Street, N.W. 20415
(202) 737-9616

MASSACHUSETTS

Boston:
3 Center Plaza 02108
(617) 223-2571

MICHIGAN

Detroit:
477 Michigan Avenue, Room 595, 48226
(313) 226-6950

MINNESOTA

Twin Cities:
Federal Building
Ft. Snelling 56111

MISSOURI

Kansas City:
Federal Building, Room 134
601 E. 12th Street 64106
(816) 374-5702

St. Louis:
Federal Building, Room 1712
1520 Market Street 63103
(314) 425-4285

NEBRASKA

Omaha:
U.S. Courthouse and Post Office Building
Room 1010, 215 N. 17th Street 68102
(402) 221-3815

NEVADA

Reno:
Mill & S. Virginia Streets
P.O. Box 3296, 89505
(702) 784-5535

NEW HAMPSHIRE

Portsmouth:
Federal Building, Room 104
Daniel & Penhallow Street 03801
(603) 436-7720 ext. 762

NEW JERSEY

Newark:
Peter W. Rodino, Jr. Federal Building
970 Broad Street 07102
(201) 645-3673

NEW MEXICO

Albuquerque:
Federal Building
421 Gold Avenue, S.W. 87102
(505) 766-5583

NEW YORK

New York City:
Jacob K. Javits Federal Building
26 Federal Plaza 10278
(212) 264-0422

Syracuse:
U.S. Courthouse and Federal Building
100 S. Clinton Street 13260
(315) 423-5660

NORTH CAROLINA

Raleigh:
Federal Building, 310 New Barn Avenue
P.O. Box 25069, 27611
(919) 756-4361

OHIO

Dayton:
Federal Building Lobby
200 W. 2nd Street 45402
(513) 225-2720 and 2854

OKLAHOMA

Oklahoma City:
200 N.W. Fifth Street, Room 206, 73102
(405) 231-4948

OREGON

Portland:
Federal Building Lobby (North)
1220 S.W. Third Street 97204
(503) 221-3141

PENNSYLVANIA

Harrisburg:
Federal Building, Room 168, 17108
(717) 782-4494

Philadelphia:
Wm. J. Green, Jr. Federal Building
600 Arch Street 19106
(215) 597-7440

Pittsburgh:
Federal Building
1000 Liberty Avenue 15222
(412) 644-2755

RHODE ISLAND

Providence:
Federal & Post Office Building, Room 310
Kennedy Plaza 02903
(401) 528-4447

TENNESSEE

Memphis:
Federal Building,
167 N. Main Street 38103
(901) 521-3956

TEXAS

Dallas:
Room 484, 1100 Commerce Street 75202
(214) 767-8035

El Paso:
First National Building, Room 1406
109 N. Oregon 79901
(915) 543-7425

Houston:
701 San Jacinto Street, 4th Floor, 77002
(713) 226-5502

San Antonio:
643 E. Durango Boulevard 78205
(512) 229-6600

VIRGINIA

Norfolk:
Federal Building, Room 220
200 Granby Mall 23610
(804) 441-3356

WASHINGTON

Seattle:
Federal Building
915 Second Avenue 98174
(206) 442-4365

WEST VIRGINIA

Charleston:
Federal Building
500 Quarrier Street 25301
(304) 343-6181 ext. 226

Other Sources

Such organizations as the Young Men's Christian Association (YMCA), the Young Women's Christian Association (YWCA) and the League of Women Voters offer many classes in adult education. Labor unions sponsor training programs for their members and many business firms make classes and on-the-job training available for their employees.

Professional associations also offer adult education. For example, it's not uncommon for a local realtor's association to offer instructional courses in buying and selling real estate. Often these courses are planned in cooperation with a community's adult-education system.

Tax Deductions for Educational Expenses

The Internal Revenue Service looks with some benevolence upon unemployed persons who are bent upon self-improvement, allowing them to list "ordinary and necessary" educational expenses as deductible items when calculating their federal income tax.

Educational expenses that go toward improving the skills you rely upon in performing the duties of your present job are those that are considered deductible. For example, if you are employed by a temporary-personnel service as a typist, and you wish to learn word processing, and you sign up at a local business school or technical institute, your tuition might be a deductible expense. The amount deducted could also include the books and supplies you purchase, and even certain travel and transportation costs. (Keep in mind that IRS rules are always subject to change.) What you pay for a correspondence course is likewise deductible, so long as the course can be judged as maintaining or improving the skills you use in performing the duties of your present job.

But educational expenses are not deductible in every case. Not included are the expenses you might incur for a training program meant to help you get a job, even though the schooling might serve to improve your skills. Suppose you're a housewife planning to return to work after several years of raising children. You sign up to take a brush-up course to improve your typing. Is the cost of the course a deductible expense? No, says the Internal Revenue Service. You must be employed in the business or profession related to your field of study in order to be eligible to take the deduction.

Government policy on this topic is outlined in detail in an IRS bulletin entitled: "Educational Expenses" (Bulletin #508), which can be obtained at your local IRS office.

As this chapter suggests, the educational programs available are rather remarkable in their number and diversity. Surely there are several in your community suited to your business or professional interests, will fit into your weekly time schedule and will not put a great strain on your budget. Becoming skilled, so vital in today's job market, is pretty much a matter of making a choice and signing up for it.

12

The Temp World—Excitement and Personal Growth

"How does one pick up the frayed threads of an early career in magazine publishing that were interrupted by 25 years as a very contented housewife and mother?" That's the question Donna Britz, a 49-year-old Skokie, Illinois, woman asked herself when her marriage suddenly fell apart and she was faced with the necessity of having to support herself.

Her daughter, who had worked for Kelly Services during her college summer vacations, supplied the answer. "Try temping; it's fun," she said. "And it's a good way to break into the job market."

"She was right on both counts," says Donna, who, after eight months of temping, found a permanent job she liked. "But it's a few other things, too. Temping can be pleasant and satisfying. It can also be scary and horrendous.

"And it's always revealing. You learn a lot about other people. You learn about yourself, too."

Donna describes one of her assignments in these

terms: "It was with a venture-capital firm. I never worked so hard in all my life. I was given rapid-fire dictation from a book on management techniques. There were no pauses. Rather than asking the man to slow down (which I later learned everyone else did), I decided to meet the challenge.

"I managed to complete it, which gave me a great deal of satisfaction. It also gave me writer's cramp and a bad case of jangled nerves.

"Later in the aternoon, the office manager asked me if I would like to return the next day. I politely declined. She then told me that the man I had worked for was upset. He wanted *me*. Not surprising. I had produced a mountain of work in less than a day's ordinary work time."

All of Donna's assignments weren't like that. "At one office where I worked, I was an assistant to the credit-manager's secretary, a lovely, darling kid, who was younger than my daughter. I gave her some tips on being assertive. That made me feel good.

"I learned a great deal from watching people, observing them," she says. "You see, for example, how different people handle the same situation or problem.

"At one office where I worked, a typist was eating a sandwich at her desk, which wasn't permitted. There was a dining area where you were supposed to have lunch or go for coffee breaks. When her boss saw her, he screamed and told her to get out of the office. She was so embarrassed she cried. It took her all day to get over the experience.

"A few weeks later at another office, the same thing happened. This time the boss grinned at the girl and said, 'Are you *that* hungry?' The girl smiled and put away the sandwich.

"The two men accomplished the same thing. But their methods were entirely different. Well, you see things like that when you temp. You learn.

"As I got better and better," Donna recalls, "many of the supervisors I worked for would put in a request with my personnel coordinator for me to return whenever the company asked for a temp.

"And I began getting job offers. I turned down several. Then one came along that I liked. It was with a magazine publisher, and I took it.

"Thinking back, I look upon temping as if it were kind of a buffet, where there are many different foods and refreshments to try. Some you don't bother with, but those you like the best, you savor."

Donna Britz's experiences as a temp are fairly typical. Through temping, a woman can explore her interests, develop her skills and prepare herself for a career that will enable her to use those skills in a meaningful way.

There's also the opportunity to develop new skills. Take 31-year-old Lynn Miller, for instance, who turned to temping when she lost her job as an executive secretary with a New York advertising agency.

One of her first assignments was at the headquarters of Home Box Office, the largest of the cable broadcasting companies. "I liked HBO from the very first day," she says. "My boss took me around and introduced me to the other people in the department. She wanted me to feel like a member of the team.

"The assignment I had was supposed to last three weeks. It stretched to five.

"Then I went back a second time, and then a third. I became a sort of permanent temp for HBO. Whenever the company needed an executive secretary, they called my service and requested me.

"There were two word processors—Vydecs—in the department where I worked. I was taught how to use them. But they weren't always available to me because other people would be using them. So I pretty much did everything on my typewriter.

"One day I had to type a very important presentation. It was a real ordeal. It took three days, twelve hours a day. I really slaved over it, but everyone thought it was terrific. When my boss's boss heard that I had done the whole presentation on a typewriter, he was very upset. He said I should have a word processor at my desk, so the company got me a Syntrex.

"Then they sent me to school to learn how to become skilled in using it. It's a fantastic machine. It saves an enormous amount of time. And it's very sophisticated. I keep going back for more training.

"I know I'm skilled and experienced enough now to be able to get all the temp work I want as a word processor. The money is very good, and I may start doing that.

"But I also have a chance to stay with HBO on a permanent basis. My boss told me in the years ahead there could be a solid career for me in cable, not as a secretary, but on an executive level. It's a field that's wide open for women because it's so new; there's no 'old boy' network.

"I'm not sure what I'm going to do right now. But it's exciting to have those options!"

The values that temping provides are very real. They not only concern skill development and career enhancement, they can also be psychological in nature. Time after time, I've seen a woman's confidence grow by leaps and bounds as she moves from one assignment to another.

There are also the benefits that can derive from the nature of the work. "When I worked as a temp," says a 37-year-old former schoolteacher, "I always requested assignments with social agencies. The office atmosphere there is usually warm and friendly. The people at these agencies, after all, are used to dealing with other people. It's not the cold corporate atmosphere you sometimes find.

"One of the agencies I worked for assisted families of mentally retarded children. These were almost exclusively low-income families.

"I started as a secretary. But, in time, I was writing the agency's newsletters, running their public relations and coordinating many of their fund-raising activities.

"I had a good deal of contact with the families we were trying to help because I had to be able to understand the work in order to be able to write about it, and inspire and motivate the people we expected to assist.

"Some of the mothers with whom we were working didn't know that a baby learned to talk by being talked to. So you'd see two-year-olds who never spoke a word.

"Through our program and services the home environment was transformed. I could see changes week by week. A kid who had been silent, sullen and lethargic would blossom, become active, play games and really babble.

"Later I was able to get a permanent position at another social service agency, but at a higher level—because of the experience I had had as a temp at the first agency.

"Members of my staff and myself are aware of many hundreds of women who have used temping to tap their potential for growing and learning. And at the same time they have used their skills and talents to prove themselves outside the home and launch satisfying careers. They have seen their marriages become revitalized and their relationships with their children improve.

"I'm not saying it's easy. I'm not saying there aren't sacrifices to be made. But the rewards are certainly worth it."

JOB DESCRIPTIONS

The pages that follow explain the principal jobs available to temp workers. The descriptions are meant to help you in requesting assignments or even in choosing areas in which to specialize and become skilled.

Your local public library is another source of information of this type. It is sure to have available several directories describing jobs and careers, including the *Occupational Outlook Handbook,* published by the U.S. Department of Labor's Bureau of Labor Statistics. The *Handbook* gives up-to-date information about several hundred occupations. For each it describes the duties and responsibilities, explains the training and qualifications needed, the prospects for advancement, working conditions, the amount of pay you can expect and current opportunities in the field (or lack of them).

As for jobs in the years ahead, the Bureau of Labor Statistics has forecast an erratic pattern of growth. The fastest growth will be among clerical workers. The number of service workers will increase, too, but not to the extent of clerical workers. (Service industries are those that provide "services," such as banking, education, health care, insurance, repair and maintenance, and transportation.) More than two-thirds of the nation's workers are employed in service industries.

Technical, managerial and administrative fields will see moderate growth during the 1980s. Farm workers and private household workers will suffer a loss of jobs.

Accounting Clerk

By any measure, accounting is a fast-growing field. American businesses and government agencies have to have basic accounting information to make major decisions. The nation's complex tax laws have spawned accounting specialists by the hundreds of thousands. And with the proliferation of computers, the demand for accountants has widened, for they are needed to prepare all the material that goes into the machines. According to the American Institute of Public Accountants, the number of working accountants in this country has tripled in the past 25 years. If it triples again before the end of the century, I would not be surprised.

The accounting clerk is usually skilled in one or more phases of accounting, such as payroll or taxes, inventory or auditing, or accounts payable and receivable.

They are found in every type of business and industry. The greatest opportunities are in urban areas where public accounting firms and the headquarter offices of large companies are found.

Qualifications: Good in arithmetic. Courses in accounting; trained in the use of accounting machines or computers for accounting operations.

Bookkeeper

New office techniques have had a profound effect on bookkeeping. This is true, however, much more in large offices than in small ones, where "hand" bookkeepers are still needed.

Bookkeepers maintain up-to-date records of accounts and business transactions in journals, ledgers and on accounting forms. They also prepare periodic statements showing money paid out and received.

In large business firms, bookkeeping is done by machine; there are many different types. Some are quite complicated and are capable of handling a wide variety of data, but most machines can be modified to record one piece of datum at a time. A good number of companies offer on-the-job training in the use of machines, but a knowledge of bookkeeping principles is required before a person begins training.

An *assistant bookkeeper* is capable of performing virtually any bookkeeping job. She or he may post and balance accounts payable, examine and code invoices and vouchers, prepare a bank reconciliation, calculate employee wages and cut payroll checks. But an assistant bookkeeper is not expected to have complete knowledge of the principles of bookkeeping. She or he knows the "how," but not necessarily the "why."

A *full-charge bookkeeper,* on the other hand, knows how to perform all bookkeeping duties and also has a thorough knowledge of bookkeeping principles.

Qualifications: Good in arithmetic; courses in principles of accounting; trained in use of bookkeeping machines or computers for bookkeeping operations.

Clerk

Although computers and various types of telecommunications equipment have revolutionized office work, the need for clerical workers has not diminished. There will always be a demand for men and women who want to sort and file and perform simple tasks on a typewriter or adding machine. The term *clerk* can refer to any one of almost a hundred different types of jobs that involve a wide variety of skills.

A clerk with basic typing skills may be asked to address envelopes, fill in addresses on invoices or perform some other simple copy-typing task. In addition, she or he is likely to file, post, answer the telephone and do all the other things clerks are asked to do.

The duties of the *file clerk* are well known. She or he must arrange papers, cards, records or even such things as reference maps and X-rays, according to an established system and locate the material again when asked to do so. Filing is usually alphabetical, chronological or numerical, although some clerks file by a particular company classification—the name of a product or job description, for example—or file geographically, as in the case of a mailing list or letters to be mailed.

Some file clerks are asked to collate. This involves arranging the individual sheets of a manuscript or booklet in their proper order. It can also involve folding and stapling the material; inserting it into envelopes, and stamping the envelopes through the use of an automatic mailing machine.

The *coding clerk* identifies particular categories of information, and codes each according to instructions she or he is given. (The evaluation test on page 79, which examines your ability to follow instructions and retain information, shows the type of work performed by the coding clerk.) The coding clerk can also be assigned to tabulate surveys, arranging information from questionnaires into different categories.

A *figure clerk* is skilled in working with a calculator or adding machine. Since putting down columns of figures is usually part of the job, legible handwriting is important.

A *mailroom clerk* sorts and distributes a company's incoming mail. Knowledge of how to operate postage meters and other mailroom equipment is usually required.

Other clerks serve as *proofreaders*, reading typed or printed material and marking errors. A knowledge of proofreading marks and symbols is necessary to do this job.

Qualifications: No special training or experience. Knowledge of simple arithmetic and ability to spell; filing skill; some typing experience and facility in operating photocopying equipment and telephone console; good penmanship. Common sense and the ability to follow company procedure; patience, a sense of order, a fondness for detail.

Computer-Operating Personnel

Computer-operating personnel are among the fastest-growing groups in the work force. They operate the electronic machines that process information and perform high-speed calculations.

Once the input for the computer has been coded, that is, prepared in a form the machine can understand (by a CRT operator or data-entry operator), it is ready for processing. A *console operator* supervises and controls the computer at this stage, starting the machine, feeding it its programmed instructions, observing that the machine functions properly and removing the completed work.

A *computer programmer* is an individual who writes the list of instructions that will be fed into or stored in the machine, which enables it to carry out its specific tasks.

Qualifications: High-school diploma; experience with data-processing equipment. Ability to think logically, to work quickly and with accuracy, plus the willingness to learn the new methods and techniques being developed almost daily.

CRT Operator; Data-Entry Operator

"The modern era of electronics has ushered in a second industrial revolution," the National Academy of Sciences has noted, "and its impact on society could be greater than that of the original industrial revolution."

Virtually every type of business activity has been touched, including the following:

Accounting	Inventory Control
Accounts Payable	Job cost Control
Accounts Receivable	Operations Research
Billing	Merchandising
Credit	Payroll
Demand Deposits (Banking)	Personnel
Direct Mail	Production Scheduling
Expenses Payable	Purchasing/Receiving
Financial Analysis	Sales Analysis
Freight Control	Sales Control
General Ledger	Warehousing
Insurance	

No matter the activity involved, all computer systems require specialized workers to enter data and instructions, a job that is performed by the *CRT operator* or *data-entry operator*. Both work at a typewriterlike keyboard before an electronic screen that displays the data they have entered.

The CRT operator has a simpler job than the data-entry operator. (CRT, which stands for "cathode ray tube," refers to the computer's screen or display terminal. The term is often used interchangeably with video-display terminal—VDT—although the two are not technically the same.) She or he may merely scan or retrieve material; there is no direct link with the computer.

People are taught the skills to operate CRT equipment through on-the-job training programs. It doesn't take long to acquire these skills. A good typist or adding machine operator shouldn't require much more than an hour or two of training.

To be a data-entry operator, special training is usually required. Many high schools now provide such training, as do business schools and adult-education programs (see Chapter 11).

As a data-entry operator, you "input" directly to

the computer, working with data-processing equipment manufactured by any one of a number of firms—IBM or Datapoint, Entrex or Digital.

Data and instructions used to be handled differently. A key-punch operator, using a machine similar to a typewriter in appearance, prepared input by punching patterns of holes in computer cards to represent specific letters, numbers and special characters. During much of the 1960s and 1970s, there was a tremendous demand for key-punch operators, but there is virtually none today.

Demonstrator

A demonstrator is a salesperson who exhibits the use or application of any one of a number of products. It can be a toy or a home appliance, a new food or a type of cosmetic. We provide demonstrators to supermarkets, department stores, and trade shows and conventions.

A good number of mature women are hired for demonstration work. "They have the look of authority," a representative of a client company once told me. "Other women respect what they say."

Qualifications: Neat appearance; articulate, outgoing; ability to speak before a group.

Health Care

Health care is an enormous and complex field. It has grown so big so fast that a major federal effort has been launched to contain its costs.

About 5 million people now work in such health-care occupations as doctor, nurse, technician and therapist. At least another million people are employed as health-care support personnel, performing the maintenance and clerical tasks associated with patient care and health facilities. Thousands more are employed in the manufacture of drugs and other health supplies.

Federal government labor specialists believe that the health industry could rank as the nation's biggest employer by the end of the decade. Temporary-personnel services have been involved in all of this. Some temp firms—New York's Medi-Temps is one—were founded precisely for the purpose of providing health-care specialists. Other temp companies furnish health-care workers along with secretaries, typists and other of the more traditional temp occupations.

The largest of the client companies in the health-care field are hospitals and nursing homes. (Before the 1930s, the nursing home was scarcely known. Today there are more than 22,000 nursing homes that employ over 700,000 workers.) In addition, health-care workers are needed by medical laboratories, family planning services, home-health services, rehabilitation centers and community mental-health centers.

Temporary-personnel services across the country provide the following health-care professionals:

Today's busy dentist relies on one or more *dental assistants*.

It's the assistant's job to work closely with the dentist: making patients comfortable; preparing them for an examination or treatment; arranging the instruments and medications; preparing solutions and mixing materials; taking and processing X-rays.

There are also clerical duties—answering telephones, receiving payment for dental services, ordering supplies and maintaining patient records.

While in some cases, the completion of an American Dental Association accredited course is required, many dental assistants learn their skills on the job. An ability to deal with people who may be under stress is another requirement.

The *home health aide* is a paraprofessional who ministers to the ill, elderly or disabled in their own homes. The duties and responsibilities of the job include assisting with bathing or giving bed baths, helping patients walk or perform prescribed exercises, checking patient pulse and respiration rates, changing surgical dressings and assisting patients with medications. An aide might also change bed linens, clean a patient's living quarters, plan and prepare meals and do food shopping.

In addition, the home health aide instructs patients and provides them with emotional support. A home health aide may teach nutrition or household management or help a person in adapting to the changes and limitations in lifestyle caused by illness or disability. During a patient's period of stress or depression, the home health aide can provide critical emotional support.

There may be a license or certification required to be a home health aide. This is a rapidly changing area and you should check for any state regulations concerning certification or license. Typically, local healthcare facilities provide the required training. This consists of a program that last from 40 to 120 hours and covers such subjects as nutrition, meal planning and preparation, plus techniques for bathing, turning and lifting patients. Other subject areas include the aging process and behavior of the elderly and the emotional problems associated with illness.

As in the case of registered nurses and other health-care specialists, a home health aide can enjoy a flexible work schedule. One requirement, however, is an automobile to be able to travel to and from patients' homes.

The *licensed practical nurse* (LPN) or *licensed vocational nurse* (LVN), works under the direction of a physician or registered nurse, providing bedside nursing care for the ill, injured, convalescent or handicapped in a medical facility or the patient's home.

In specific terms, the licensed practical nurse takes and records patients' temperatures, blood pressure and pulse and respiration rates, gives injections, changes surgical dressings and administers prescribed medication, recording the time and dosage. The LPN may also help patients dress, walk and bathe.

Often the LPN assists in patient and family rehabilitation by providing emotional support, teaching self-care techniques and suggesting the use of community resources. Many work in specialized activities, such as obstetrics, pediatrics, coronary care, intensive care or in the operating, recovery or emergency rooms.

Thousands of women re-entering the work force have become LPNs. It takes anywhere from a year to 18 months. A high-school diploma is usually the basic requirement. You sign up for a state-approved course at a local community college, vocational or technical school, or hospital or health agency. After completing the course, you take a state licensing examination. (The National Federation of Licensed Practical Nurses warns against correspondence courses, which are not likely to qualify a candidate to take the state licensing exam.)

Your training program covers anatomy, physiology, pediatrics, psychiatric nursing, administration of drugs, nutrition and first aid. You also get experience working with patients.

Besides the vocational training, being a licensed practical nurse requires a special temperament. "You have to have a deep concern for people and their well-being," says one nursing director. "And it takes a really stable person. After all, you're around people who are sick and injured, and that can be very upsetting when you do it day after day."

The *nurse's aide,* working under the direction of the nursing staff, assists in patient care. The job can also be called hospital attendant, nursing assistant or orderly.

The nurse's aide bathes and dresses patients, serves food, feeds patients requiring assistance, assists patients in walking and responds to patients' signal lights or bed calls.

The nurse's aide also takes and records temperatures, pulses and perspiration rates; gives massages, applies compresses and holds instruments and positions lights during examinations.

To work as a nurse's aide, a candidate must be at least 17 years old and have completed eight years of education. Health-care facilities conduct on-the-job training programs that last from several weeks to three or four months. Emotional stability and a deep-seated desire to help people are other requirements.

Of the approximately 5 million persons employed in the health-care field, about one-half are *registered nurses* (RN). Despite their number, the demand for nurses currently exceeds the supply in most parts of the country, particularly in inner-city areas and some southern states. About 70 percent of all registered nurses work full time; 30 percent are part-time or temp employees.

The registered nurse not only administers prescribed drugs and provides other medication, assists in examinations, prepares instruments and equipment for use, but she (94 percent of all nurses are women) is also playing an increasingly important role in observing patient progress and assessing the efficacy of prescribed treatment. The registered nurse is also responsible for supervising licensed practical nurses, nurse's aides and other auxiliary health-care workers.

Most nurses are employed as hospital-staff nurses, providing direct patient care. But others are in private duty, and serve in public health, industrial or school nursing, or work in physicians' offices or nursing homes. There are also gerontological nurses, occupational health nurses, medical-surgical nurses, obstetrical and pediatric nurses and psychiatric and mental-health nurses.

A license is required to practice professional nursing. In order to qualify for a license, the applicant must fulfill the requirements for a Bachelor's Degree in nursing, complete a two-year associate degree program at a junior or community college, or complete a two- or three-year program at a hospital school of nursing. Anatomy, physiology, microbiology, nutrition and psychology are among the subjects studied. Passing a licensing exam is required by many states.

Merchandising, Marketing Aide

These categories cover many different types of jobs. Indeed, no two assignments in the field are likely to be the same.

Temporary workers are often used in market research, conducting telephone or personal surveys, sometimes offering samples of a product to determine whether individuals are pleased with the package design or the product itself. Then, in a related function, they process the results of such activity, sorting premium coupons as they are received, typing labels, mailing the premiums, etc.

Temps are often used to staff exhibits at conventions and trade shows, greeting visitors, registering guests and distributing brochures. They demonstrate products in supermarkets and department stores. They pass out sample products on city streets.

Temps are sent out by companies to do comparison shopping, canvassing retail outlets to determine what competitors are charging for goods. They may even be assigned to scrutinize a retail outlet operated by a client company to check clerks for appearance and attitude.

Most of these assignments are with advertising agencies or independent research organizations.

Qualifications: Articulate and outgoing; relaxed with people. Good grooming; neat appearance. Retail sales experience is helpful.

Receptionist

The receptionist greets customers and other visitors and directs them to the appropriate person. Most receptionists work for firms that provide business or personnel services, but they also are employed in the medical field, by dentists and doctors, by hospitals and nursing homes.

Virtually all receptionists perform other duties besides greeting visitors. They operate telephone consoles, do light typing, keep records or file.

Qualifications: Typing and clerical skills; ability to operate telephone console. Good appearance, pleasant voice, even disposition; desire to be helpful and informative.

Sales Assistant

Temporary services, particularly the larger firms, provide retail establishments with salespeople to augment their regular sales staffs. The work is usually seasonal. Department stores, discount stores, appliance stores and toy stores have a critical need for additional help in the weeks before Christmas, Easter and in connection with special sales.

No special training is necessary. You make out sales or charge slips, receive cash payments and give out change and receipts. In the case of a small store, you might also stock shelves, mark price tags and prepare displays.

Temps also perform a variety of sales-related jobs. These include such activities as checking or setting up product displays in retail locations, providing improved shelf display for a customer's product, or inventorying the merchandise a retail outlet has in stock, then reporting the results along with a recommendation as to what should be reordered.

Note to moonlighters: Retail sales work is available not only on a 9 A.M.-to-5 P.M. basis, but also in the evening and on weekends.

Qualifications: High-school diploma is preferred; ability to work with figures. Previous sales experience is a plus factor but not a necessity; on-the-job training is usually provided. Good appearance; pleasant, amiable personality; ability to be at ease with people.

Secretary; Stenographer

"A qualified professional secretary need never be unemployed, no matter the state of the economy," a spokesperson for Professional Secretaries International declared not long ago. It's true. While American business and government agencies are churning out more paperwork than ever before, the number of secretaries has been steadily declining. The need is very great.

Generally, a *secretary* processes and transmits information. In a typical secretarial job, you type, take dictation, file, answer telephones, place calls and operate office machines, perhaps a calculator or a teletype machine. You also perform some clerical tasks, such as filing, photocopying and handling incoming mail.

A *stenographer* takes dictation in shorthand or by means of a variety of recording machines. The dictation usually involves correspondence or reports, but sometimes the stenographer is asked to transcribe the proceedings of a meeting or executive conference. The stenographer is one of a group, or "pool," and may be required to take dictation from several different individuals in the course of a week.

A stenographer in the temporary-help field seldom does any clerical work. Taking dictation and typing are 95 percent of the job.

An *executive secretary* is one with the skills of a general secretary, but who functions as an administrative assistant to a company VIP. The executive secretary is likely to have the authority to plan office routines and schedule appointments and meetings. Supervising clerical employees is another responsibility the executive secretary may have.

Temporary-help services place many different types of specialized secretaries. The *legal secretary* is skilled in the use of a legal vocabulary and has a knowledge of standard legal forms. Legal secretaries are assigned to law firms, corporation offices and trade associations. The *medical secretary* has to be knowledgeable in the use of medical terms and be informed as to medical-office procedures. Hospitals and clinics, insurance companies, public-health facilities and firms that manufacture or distribute medical supplies require medical secretaries.

The work of the *technical secretary* is usually related to a particular field of engineering—aeronautical, civil, electronic, mechanical or chemical. The dictated material often involves technical terms, equations and formulas and sometimes statistical information.

The *bilingual secretary* is capable of taking dictation in one other language besides English. The bilingual secretary is often hired by import-export agencies, travel agencies and multinational corporations. A perfect knowledge of the second language is required.

About two-thirds of all secretaries are placed in

banks, insurance companies, real-estate firms, advertising agencies and other business firms.

For years, secretaries were almost exclusively female. That began to change in the 1960s. The number of male secretaries, while growing slightly, is not yet significant.

Qualifications: High-school diploma or business school certificate is preferred, plus a knowledge of spelling, punctuation and grammar; good vocabulary. Superior skills in typing and shorthand. A "junior" secretary or stenographer should be able to take dictation at the rate of 80 to 100 words per minute, and type at the rate of 40 to 50 words per minute. In the case of an experienced secretary or stenographer a dictation speed of 100 to 120 words per minute and a typing speed of 50 to 60 words per minute are expected.

Switchboard Operator

Working with a call director, or even more elaborate equipment, such as that manufactured by Centrex, Horizons or Dimensions, the switchboard operator connects interoffice calls, answers and relays incoming calls, assists company callers in making outgoing calls and supplies information to callers. The switchboard operator may also act as a receptionist and do simple clerical tasks, such as mail sorting or light typing.

Qualifications: Clear and pleasant voice; ability to remain seated for long periods and sometimes work rapidly under pressure.

Telephone Solicitor

A telephone solicitor places calls to prospective customers from a list provided by the client company, explains the merchandise or service being offered, quotes prices and takes orders. Many different companies use telephone solicitation, including those selling insurance, real estate and magazine or newspaper subscriptions. Even lawn care is now sold by telephone.

We place women and men in telephone solicitation jobs on a year-round basis. Most of the assignments are for evening work.

Qualifications: Good speaking voice; glibness, persistence.

Teletype (Telex) Operator

The teletype machine is a telegraphic apparatus with a keyboard which resembles that of a typewriter. By striking the letters and symbols, you transmit messages to distant points where they are received and reproduced by a similar machine.

A skilled teletype operator can send messages, receive them (interpreting the coded symbols) and also make minor repairs on the machines.

In some firms, teletype machines must be manned around the clock because they are linked to international stations. This means late-evening and early-morning work is available.

Qualifications: On-the-job experience is required.

Typist

Good typists are needed by every type of business. If you are skilled as a typist, you never need to be unemployed.

But versatility can be important. A typist who is capable of operating several different types of electric and manual machines, cutting stencils, and laying out and typing statistical tables and other kinds of unwieldy material has a greater choice of jobs and is better paid than the typist whose skills are limited to addressing envelopes.

There are several different typing specialities. A *copy typist* "copies" material from printed or typewritten drafts or handwritten notes and types it out in final form. Working from a printed or typewritten list of addresses, the copy typist might fill out printed forms or type headings on form letters. Cutting stencils or multilith plates are other tasks sometimes performed by the copy typist.

A *manuscript typist,* working from an author's copy of his work—which is likely to bear copyreader's symbols indicating word and letter additions, deletions and transpositions—must produce a perfect draft, ready for the printer.

The work of the *statistical typist* is similar to that of the copy typist, except that it involves numbers and numerical data, usually in column form. An experienced statistical typist can take an accountant's handwritten draft of a balance sheet or profit-and-loss statement, and, in laying out and typing it, space and arrange the statistics so they all apear in perfect alignment.

The *transcription typist* transcribes dictation from recordings produced on tapes, disks or belts. Some transcription typists specialize, that is, they become legal, medical or technical typists.

Other specialties are *invoice typists* and *policy typists*. The latter fill in the blanks of insurance policies.

Qualifications: High-school diploma or business school certificate is preferred; knowledge of office procedures; neatness; accuracy. A typing speed of 40 words per minute is considered adequate; 50 to 55 is average (and required by most temp services to be designated as being skilled) and 60 to 80 is above average. The ability to operate adding machines, duplicating machines, copiers and other types of equipment enhance a typist's value.

Word Processor

As noted earlier in this book, there has been a dramatic increase in the demand for women and men who are skilled in the use of word processors. By the early 1980s, the demand about equalled that for typists, according to Marty Orenstein, president of Good People temporaries, one of New York's leading temp services specializing in office automation. By the end of the decade, it is certain to surpass it.

The Association of Information Systems Professionals classifies those with word-processing skills as follows:

A *word-processing trainee* is an individual with 0 to 12 months of word-processing experience. A trainee should be able to type at a speed of 50 to 60 words per minute, have a good knowledge of grammar, punctuation, spelling and formatting; the ability to use dictionaries, handbooks and other reference materials and be oriented toward teamwork and the use of machines.

A trainee's duties include routine transcription and manipulation of text from various types of source information (dictation, handwriting, etc.). The trainee is also expected to maintain production records and perform some proofreading.

A *word-processing operator* is an individual with 6 to 24 months of word-processing experience. In addition to having all the functions of a trainee, the word-processing operator handles special documents, meets established quality standards, uses all of a machine's text-editing functions and is familiar with department terminology and company practices.

Among the jobs that have evolved out of word processing, are *word-processing administrative secretary* and *word-processing supervisor*. The word-processing administrative secretary is a position with a good deal of responsibility, requiring an individual of intelligence and good judgment. The word-processing administrative secretary, working for a company VIP, plans office routines, schedules appointments and meetings, greets clients and visitors, supervises clerical workers and, generally, coordinates the VIP's work flow.

The word-processing administrative secretary may have a word-processing terminal at her or his desk, or assigns work to a word-processing operator or the word-processing department or center.

In many large companies, the word-processing staff is organized into word-processing centers, where several operators are assigned. A word-processing supervisor is responsible for each center, taking work requests from company managers and parceling them out to the operators. It's the supervisor's responsibility to coordinate the work flow and check completed documents. She or he also advises and assists the operators.

Glossary

Assign: To place a temp employee with a client company.

Assignment: The period of time a temp employee works for a client company.

Balanced staffing: To supplement a company's permanent work force with temporary employees during peak-work periods.

Client company: The firm to which temporary employees are assigned after being hired by the temp service.

Job sharing: A type of permanent employment in which two employees hold one full-time position.

Part time: Being employed on a regular basis, but working less than full time.

Permanent, perm: A person who is employed on a full-time basis.

Personnel coordinator: The individual at a temp service who interviews and assigns.

Temp, temp employee: An employee of a temp service who is assigned to work on the premises of one of the service's client companies.

Temping: Being employed as a temp.

Temporary-personnel service: A company that assigns temporary employees to assist its customers in handling special projects, peak periods, vacation and sick-leave fill-ins.